Book 1
Circuit Engineering
By Solis Tech

&

Book 2
Quality Assurance
By Solis Tech

Book 1
Circuit Engineering
By Solis Tech

The Beginner's Guide to Electronic Circuits, Semi-Conductors, Circuit Boards, and Basic Electronics

Circuit Engineering: The Beginner's Guide to Electronic Circuits, Semi-Conductors, Circuit Boards and Basic Electronics

Circuit Engineering: The Beginner's Guide to Electronic Circuits, Semi-Conductors, Circuit Boards and Basic Electronics

Table of Contents

Introduction

I want to thank you and congratulate you for purchasing the book, **Circuit Engineering: The Beginner's Guide to Electronic Circuits, Semi-Conductors, Circuit Boards, and Basic Electronics**.

This book contains a beginner's course on circuit engineering. Here, the basics of electric and electronic circuits are discussed. You will grasp the definitions of circuits, semi-conductors, resistors, inductors, transformers, circuit boards, and electronics, in general. You'll even be introduced to electrical safety tips and a set of skills needed in electronics, as well as a short take on reverse engineering, hacking, microcontroller programming, and robotics.

Alongside, you can apply all that you'll be learning once you get started with the proposed circuit projects for beginner. You'll also be rewarded a peek at different career-advancement possibilities. While reading about the fundamentals and various theories in the subject is important, hands-on learning is equally important. This way, you can put your newly gathered knowledge to good use.

If you're uncertain whether or not you have what it takes to learn the ropes in circuit engineering, let this book help you decide. Chances are, you have the stamina for the field and for all you know, you can discover a new passion for circuits and electronic devices.

Thanks again for purchasing this book; I hope you enjoy it!

Chapter I – First Things First: An Introduction to Circuit Engineering

In 1882, there was a *circuit war*; it was between the notable electrical engineers and scientists, *Thomas Edison* (inventor of the DC system) and *Nikola Tesla* (inventor of the AC system).

While Thomas Edison stated that an efficient way of distributing power was via a *DC system*, Nikola Tesla argued that although DC systems are efficient, an *alternating current* is the *more practical* option. It started as a simple clash of ideas, but it eventually led to a major rift. Neither professional conceded; both of them insisted that their own systems were "better".

In the end, it was *Nikola Tesla* that took home the *glory*. Case in point? He was granted funds by an internationally recognized firm, Westinghouse. The majority of the power sources of New York City were based on the ideas of the Serbian engineer; at Niagara Falls in Canada, a power plant was built.

If you're interested in finding out more about the particular *circuit war, AC and DC systems*, and all critical discussions on circuits, taking a course about electronic circuits is the way to go.

I.A. - What Is a Circuit?

Both an *electric circuit* and an *electronic circuit* refer to a complete pathway for electric current, which starts and ends at a single point; it is a passage that allows the electricity to enter at one place, then, let it pass through a series of stops, and finally, leave it to exit at the same place. The list of basic examples of a circuit includes a *light switch* (off and on) and *battery-operated lamps*.

A circuit that follows a fundamental design

A circuit can function well - granted that its design is well-conceptualized. As much as possible, it is recommended that arriving at a simplistic product should be the goal; the simple and straightforward a design is, the better. With a fundamental concept, even if other (beginner-level) circuit engineers who will subject it to inspection will not have a difficult time in understanding its flow. Although there may be complex systems, the agenda is not intended to complicate the explanations.

Moreover, a circuit can be referred to as a space with a conductive path that grants electrons the opportunity to move freely. To create one with a brilliant design, a tip is to learn about the classifications of all circuits. You can use the knowledge to determine the appropriate kind of network, as well as the need for an external or internal source.

2 classifications of a circuit:

1. Linear or non-linear – a circuit that is based on either linear or non-linear networks; it is composed of independent and/or dependent sources and passive elements

2. Active or passive – a circuit that is based on either the absence (passive circuit) or the presence (active circuit) of a source; a source can be a power source or voltage source

I.B. - A Circuit & Its Types

Not all circuits are alike. In fact, one of the most common misconceptions involves an *electric circuit* and an *electronic circuit*; both are said to be one and the same, but they are not. While the former can carry *average to high voltage*, the latter has the tendency to have *low voltage load*.

Moreover, it is always important to be aware of the different circuit types, especially if you're about to make your own circuit; the kind of circuit that you create needs to have the ability to handle a preferred load.

Circuit types:

- Closed circuit – it is a circuit that is fully functional

- Open circuit – it is a circuit that can no longer function due to a damaged or missing component, or a loose connection

- Short circuit – it is a circuit that comes without a load

- Parallel circuit – it is a circuit that connects to other circuits; it is like the main power source or the primary circuit in a series of circuits

- Series circuit – it is a circuit that connects to other circuits; the same amount of electricity is distributed to each of its component circuits; the main power source or the primary circuit is unclear

I.C. - Conductors, Insulators & Semi-Conductors

Conductors, insulators, and *semi-conductors* give light to the fact that a circuit's electrical properties are dependent on the circuit type, as well as on their conduction bands (i.e. their allowed electric power). For instance, if a particular power source chooses to distribute a 9-volt electric power to a closed circuit, its electrical properties can be evaluated by using 2 details: (1) its characteristic as a closed circuit and (2) 9-volt electric power.

Moreover, conductors, insulators, and semi-conductors are integral concepts to the *conductivity* of an object. While conductors and semi-conductors are grouped to describe *charged carriers*, insulators are still considered as relative despite not containing any free charge.

Circuit Engineering: The Beginner's Guide to Electronic Circuits, Semi-Conductors, Circuit Boards and Basic Electronics

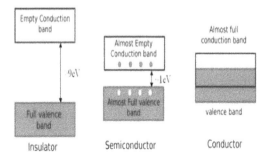

Insulators can be any "ion-less" object; the most common examples of semi-conductors are copper and aluminum & for conductors, gold and silver

Conduction bands:

- Conductor – it is a conduction band that is referred to as the almost full band

- Insulator – it is a conduction band that is referred to as an empty band

- Semi-conductor – it is a conduction band that is referred to as an almost empty band

I.D. - Breaking Down the Components of a Circuit

A circuit can be either *simple or complex,* and be both *simple and complex.* If the circuit in subject is a series circuit, with a group of 10 different circuits that are connected to it or if the said circuit is just a basic closed circuit with 5 different stops, it can be rather confusing to trace. However, if you dissect any circuit, you'll discover 3 *constant,* integral components.

Integral components:

1. Load – it is the representation of the power consumption, as well as the work that is accomplished within a system; without it, there's barely a point in having a circuit

2. Power source – it is where the electricity comes from

3. Pathway – it is the framework of a circuit; from the power source, it follows the load through each of the network, and finally returns to

and exits the power source; it is also referred to as the conductive pathway

I.E. - The Roles of Current, Resistance & Voltage

Current, resistance, and voltage are the 3 representations of the important components of a circuit's system. They can explain how electricity enters, then, moves from 1 point to another, and finally exits. Whether the path of electricity is rather simple, these representations remain constant. Apart from describing the electric flow, they can serve as indications of faults (in instances when a circuit fails to work).

3 representations:

- Current – it is the representation of the electric flow; particularly, its focus is on the flow of electrons

- Resistance – it is the representation of the nature of an electric flow as it moves around the circuit

- Voltage – it is the representation of the electric force or pressure; in general, the supply comes from an electric outlet or a battery

I.F. - AC/DC Systems: Which System Is in?

AC and DC systems (or alternating current and direct current systems) are often associated to each other. When the *AC system* is mentioned, so is the *DC system*. Conversely, when it's the DC system's turn to be in the spotlight, it won't be long until the AC system is mentioned. This is because these systems are opposite of one another; to get a better understanding of one of them, it's recommended to be familiar with the other, as well.

Moreover, *AC and DC systems* are types of a circuit's current flow. In an AC system, the current flow changes its direction occasionally. Meanwhile, in a DC system, the current flow follows a single direction.

It can be deduced, therefore, that an AC system grants a circuit freedom to let the current flow in several directions. While this can be an advantage, this doesn't permit the continuous flow that a DC system can entitle.

So, should you use an *AC system* or a *DC system*? The decision as to which current system is dependent on the more practical design to follow; take into account the aim of having your own circuit. If you prefer something grand and you intend to power something large, the AC system can step in. On the other hand, if you're good with a basic setup, you can use the DC system's concept as basis.

I.G. – What Is a Transformer?

A *transformer* is a device that serves as a portal for energy transfer within the points in a circuit or from circuit 1 to circuit 2. In most cases, it is used for increasing and decreasing the voltages in a system.

When the first transformer was built in the mid 1880s, circuit engineers discovered that a transformer significantly improves the electric flow in a circuit, and consequently, results to a more powerful circuit. The discovery made way for various transformer designs, as well as various transformer sizes.

A primary principle of a transformer is its need for extremely *high magnetic permeability*. It follows that a circuit that is capable of attracting power is, of course, more inclined to have electric current transferred to it; and, conversely, a circuit with *low magnetic permeability* is less likely to extract power from another circuit.

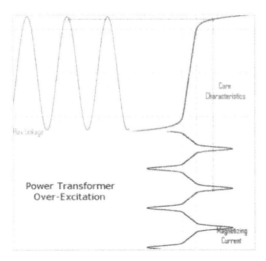

Magnetic permeability is defined as the ability of a circuit to hold and support an internal magnetic field

Chapter II – The Anatomy of a Circuit

Let's say that a lamp in your room has been around for a while, and let's say it chose to give up on you the other night; although it's an old lamp, you still believe it can *work fine*. You suspect that the problem is in the switching board. Instead of just letting it be and since you're interested in how it works, you choose to study its components.

As you open its internal system, you see that connected to some sort of panel are 2 wires; one wire is red, the other is black. As far as your knowledge in circuits can tell you, the 2 wires in your hands are: (1) a live wire or the wire that is connected to a switch, and (2) a neutral wire or the wire that carries the load.

As the universal rule in circuit engineering goes, *red* is the color that indicates a live wire, *black*, on the other hand, is a neutral wire. For a chance to know why your lamp gave up on you other than old age, checking the red wire would be a good start.

II.A. – Individually Speaking: Parts of a Circuit

A circuit can *work smoothly* if its individual parts are contributing to the workflow as expected. Remember that it follows a series; if one point in that series is not in condition. So, if you're wondering why a system is functional, check each one of its components. To use the old adage (and modify it a bit), the circuit, as a whole, is just as good as its individual parts.

Individual parts:

- Capacitor – it is in charge of the stability in the power source in a circuit

- Diode – it is in charge of supplying the light in a circuit

- Inductor – it is a coil of wiring system

- Resistor – it is in charge of power consumption

- Transistor – it is in charge of the electric signal control

II.B. – Circuit Categories: Which Category Do You Belong to?

Circuit categories describe the *voltage levels*, as well as their *electric flow over time*; they refer to how much and how powerful the current is as it enters and passes through each point in a circuit. Since they vary, it's listed as an effective way of understanding circuit systems of sorts if they are categorized.

Circuit categories:

- Analog circuits – these are the categories of circuits that use the concepts of parallel circuits and series circuits as basis. Among their fundamental parts are capacitors, diodes, resistors, and wires.

  In diagrams, analog circuits are easy to recognize. Usually, when a model of the particular circuit is drawn, a simple illustration is presented since these circuits do not follow a complex system. In most cases, when illustrated, the parts (e.g. capacitors, diodes, wires, etc.) are represented by lines.

- Digital circuits – these are the circuits that rely heavily on Boolean algebra (i.e. values are either true or false, or as denoted 1 or 0); therefore, these circuits are often dependent on transistors that can create closed logic. Compared to analog circuits, these follow a state-of-the-art design.

  Furthermore, digital circuits are designed to create either numerical or logical values for the representation of electricity that flows within their system. Since these are not only focused on the mere ability to take in electric current, but rather, on the individual properties of all of their parts, as well, these circuits come with advanced functions; they can provide memory and accomplish arbitrary computations.

- Analog-digital – these circuits are sometimes called hybrid circuits or mixed signal circuits since both system designs of analog and digital circuits are given light. Although their concept can be quite complex, these circuits can deliver a more thorough result; the procedures are combined, which allows collaborative effort from different parts. One example is a telephone receiver; first, it works based on analog circuitry to create and stabilize signals, then, based on digital circuitry, these signals are converted into digital units, and finally, are subjected to interpretation.

II.C. – Where Does Inductance Enter the Picture?

In circuit analysis, the term *inductance*, introduced in 1886 by *Oliver Heaviside*, refers to the property of a circuit's electricity-producing component to change in amount. Apart from the support of a circuit's aspect to vary, it points out the need for a filter and energy storage systems to be provided.

As it follows, the component in a circuit that enables inductance is called an inductor. Usually, these parts are made out of wire. But, while some circuits contain inductors as integral parts, others remain functional without the need to alter the electric flow.

Inductance can be either *mutual inductance* or *self-inductance*. The former refers to a change in electric current from one inductor to another inductor; it explains the primary operations of a transformer. Meanwhile, the latter refers to the *stable inductance* within a system.

Moreover, inductance is represented by the symbol *L*, which is meant to giver to the scientist, *Heinrich Lenz*. It also measured in units of *henry* after the American scientist, *Joseph Henry*; it follows that although it was Oliver Heaviside who introduced the term, the man behind the development is Joseph Henry.

Mutual inductance describes the occurrence in a circuit when there is change that can be traced to an inductor; particularly, it refers to the alteration due to an inductor's preference of a nearby inductor. It is essential to learn about the relationship of *2 inductors* since it is the basis of the operations of a transformer. Additionally, a limit has to be maintained in order to keep potential energy transfers regulated; the failure to incorrectly calculate mutual inductance can result to *unwanted inductance coupling*, as well as a *power overload*.

It can, therefore, be deduced that mutual inductance (as represented by the symbol *M*) is the measurement of the coupling that involves 2 inductors; the 2 inductors are, then, given particular importance (in terms of coil turns), along with each inductor's ability to admit current flow or *permeance*. The formula for calculating mutual inductance is as follows:

**representations: M_{AB} = mutual inductance in circuit A and circuit B

N_B = inductance in circuit B

N_A = inductance in circuit A

P_{AB} = permeability in circuit A and circuit B

$M_{AB} = (N_B)(N_A)(P_{AB})$

When explained, the formula highlights that the mutual inductance between inductor A and inductor B (or M_{AB}) is equal to the product of 3 elements: [1] the coils of inductor B (or N_B), [2] the coils of inductor A (or N_A), and [3] the permeance of inductor A and inductor B (or P_{AB}).

On the other hand, self-inductance refers to voltage induction of a current-carrying system in respect to the changing current in the circuit. It points out that eventually, there will be another current that will flow along with the primary current. Due to the amount of force within the magnetic field, voltage is induced; particularly, voltage is *self-induced*.

II.D. - What Makes an Integrated Circuit?

An *integrated circuit* (or IC) is alternatively called a microchip or a chip, due to its size. It works depending on a particular signal level. One example is the integrated circuit that enables a computer to perform a multitude of tasks; instead of loading a computer's structure with a large circuit, it comes to the rescue.

In most cases, an *integrated circuit* operates at little defined states. Compared to the normal circuit whose operations are distributed over continuous amplitudes, it can function within a small network; the normal circuit may sometimes fail to work with only minor amplitude ranges.

Basically, an *integrated circuit* is no different from any other circuit; its power can astound you, yes, but, if it comes down to describing how it is, it's simply a circuit that has been reduced so it can fit inside a chip.

Chapter III – Resistance Isn't Futile

Without a material that can act as the opposing force, a circuit can *function*, but it may not function *as desired*. When an electric supply can perform its function by distributing electricity to the opening of a circuit, the electric current will keep on flowing; its flow can be uncontrollable, which can destroy a system's integrity. Usually, without the opposition, a circuit ends up taking too much load.

The term for this opposing material is *resistance*; it goes hand in hand with the term conductance. And, as mentioned in the first chapter, it is the representation of the current flow in a circuit.

III.A. – What Is Resistance?

Resistance is the measurement of an opposing electric current; it can be expressed in ohms. It generates an amount of friction that is relative to the necessary amount of electricity that a particular circuit can handle.

In a way, *resistance* is responsible for the *smooth flow of electricity* in a circuit. Although others would counter the argument by saying that rather than support the effortless flow of electricity in a system, it slows it down.

However, it is *resistance* that allows *balance of electricity* in a circuit. Take for example the case of a circuit that can only handle a total of 15V. If a circuit takes in 20V at a resistance of 5 ohms, the number is diminished to 15V, which indicates a functional circuit. Conversely, if, in the same situation, there is no *resistance* of 5 ohms, a circuit may not be as functional as desired; its system ends up carrying 20V, which implies that it is overloaded.

III.B. – Resistive Circuit 101

A *resistive circuit* is a kind of circuit that consists of nothing but a series of resistors to complete the combo of electric current and voltage source. If viewed in a chart, it is noticeable that the power waveform is always positive; it is suggestive the power in a circuit is always dissipated, and is never returned to the original source.

It is important to note that the frequency of the power in a circuit should not be equal to the frequency of the electric current and voltage. If possible, the frequency of the power should be twice as high as that of the electric current and voltage. This unequal frequency distribution grants constant change within a system.

Since it is made up of resistors and does not include transistors and capacitors, a resistive circuit is rather easier to analyze. Understanding the electric flow within the circuit (whether in an AC or DC system) requires a straightforward technique. Therefore, determining the flow of the current in a resistive circuit is simple; by adhering to the formula, calculating the figure is easy.

In a resistive circuit, voltage can easily be monitored

**representations: I = total current

RS = Resistance Source

RL = Resistance Load

I = voltage ÷ (RS +RL)

III.C. - War between the Types of Resistance

Resistance is classified according to the type of resistivity that it can contain, along with the amount of resistance that a circuit can carry. This allows the opportunity for an opposing force to be valued, regardless of its resistivity. As the professional electrical engineers can attest, not every circuit component that produces resistance satisfies the rules, particularly, *Ohm's Law*.

2 types of resistance:

- Differential resistance – it is the resistance derivative of voltage in light with the electric current; also referred to as *incremental resistance, small signal resistance, or dynamic resistance*, its concept is responsible for oscillators and amplifiers

17

- Static resistance – it is the resistance that corresponds to the typical definition of resistance; it is also called *chordal resistance* or *DC resistance*

III.D. - Resistance vs. Conductance

The average circuit comes with both *resistance* and *conductance*, which gives balance to the electric flow in a circuit's system. While the former refers to the opposition, conductance describes the amount of current that is converted into power that revolves around different points.

Conductance also covers the ability of a circuit's components to conduct electricity. And, to bring light to its counterpart's ability to oppose the flow, it dwells on the subject of the convenience of electricity to pass through a series of points in a circuit.

With both the resistance and the conductance in the system, a circuit can function as desired.

III.E. – The Need for Calculations (Four Ways)

For electric current to flow smoothly within a system, a level of resistance has to be present. And, since not all circuits come with a similar design, their resistance levels vary. To calculate a particular circuit's resistance, first, you need determine its type, and its provided values, as well.

Four ways:

#1 – Resistance calculation for a series circuit

The formula:

Resistance = $_1R + _2R + _3R + _4R$

#2 – Resistance calculation according to voltage & power

**representations: total voltage; PT = total power

The formula:

Resistance = $VT^2 \div PT^2$

3 – Resistance calculation according to voltage & current

**representations: VT = total voltage; IT = total current

The formula:

Resistance = VT ÷ IT

4 – Resistance calculation according to power & current

**representations: PT = total power; IT = total current

The formula:

Resistance = PT ÷ IT

III.F. – What about Sheet Resistance?

Sheet resistance refers to the measurement of the resistance in a thin sheet in a circuit's components. It can be used to describe the resistibility of different circuits and can point out the specific difference in circuits that vary in size. Especially in the case of a commercial product, the topic is covered for the assurance of quality.

You can look at *sheet resistance* as a special kind of resistance since it generates a more specific value. Usually, the average resistance in a circuit is expressed in *ohms*; *sheet resistance* is expressed in *Ohms per square*.

In most cases, *sheet resistance* is used for the analysis of circuits with uniform conductivity or semi-conductivity. Typical applications are extended to quality assurance for a commercial circuit.

III.G. – The Role of Impedance & Admittance

Like resistance, *impedance* can be described as the opposition in a circuit; unlike resistance, however, it refers to the opposing force of a circuit after the application of voltage. It is only relevant to AC systems or circuits where direct current isn't the supplied.

It was in 1893 when the concept of *impedance* was initially introduced by the Irish engineer, Arthur Kenelly. Back then, it was denoted by Z and is defined as a complex number.

When it comes to quantitative terms, *impedance* refers to the ratio of voltage to the electric current in a circuit. Its introduction is important for beginners especially if they're scratching their heads as to why there's an opposing force besides resistance.

Impedance, like resistance, comes with values. In a single open circuit, its value is presented in *ohms*. In the event of a series circuit or a parallel circuit, its value can be calculated by simply adding all the defined values in each unit.

The formula:

**representations: TZ = total impedance

Z_1 = impedance in component 1

Z_2 = impedance in component 2

Z_3 = impedance in component 3

Z_{10} = impedance in final component of a circuit

$$TZ = Z_1 + Z_2 + Z_3 \ldots Z_n$$

Meanwhile, *admittance* is a relative concept in circuit engineering. It addresses the issue that alongside the difference in the magnitude of the electric current and voltage that are flowing within a circuit, the difference in phases needs to be given light, too. This way, the maximum load within a system can be calculated accordingly.

The formula:

**representations: TY = total admittance

Y_1 = admittance in component 1

Y_2 = admittance in component 2

Y_3 = admittance in component 3

Y_{10} = admittance in final component of a circuit

$$TY = Y_1 + Y_2 + Y_3 \ldots Y_n$$

Chapter IV – It's Time to Measure the Electric Flow in a Circuit

In the previous chapter, the formulas for the calculation of a circuit's resistance levels were shared. However, the formulas for the *calculation of the entire load* in a circuit have yet to be discussed.

This is due to the significance of using the appropriate measurement units. In a few cases, especially those who are still on the initial phase of learning circuits? They aren't quite careful with their selected units. As it follows, it's not only necessary to calculate a circuit's electric flow; it's also necessary to calculate a circuit's flow correctly.

IV.A. – Standard Units

Among the several reasons to use *standard units of measurement* are for indications of exact measurements and for indications of the preferred measurements in a system. These units bring uniformity.

In circuits, the usual standard units that you encounter are *V, W, I,* and *P.* Although there are more, those who wish to explain a system's electric flow rely on these measurements; rather than introduce a bunch, which may only make matters more confusing, some are preferred. Moreover, without such units, understanding others' discussions of circuits is nearly impossible.

Standard units:

- Conductance – its measuring unit is Siemen with G as symbol

- Current – its measuring unit is ampere with I or i as symbol

- Frequency – its measuring unit is Hertz with Hz as symbol

- Inductance – its measuring unit is Henry with H or L as symbol

- Power – its measuring is watts with W as symbol

- Resistance – its measuring unit is ohm with R as symbol

- Voltage – its measuring unit is volt with V or E as symbol

IV.B. – Commonly Used Alternatives

Other than the *standard units of measurement*, other units are given light since these can enable clearer expression of the electric flow in a circuit. Especially if the circuit in subject contains a rather complex system, it can be difficult to arrive at a definite solution.

Other units:

- Angular frequency – it is a unit of measurement used in an AC circuit; it is a rotational unit that describes the relationship of at least 2 electric forms in a circuit

- Decibel – it is a unit of measurement that represent the gain in either current, power, or voltage; since it is only a tenth of the original unit, *Bel*, it is primarily reserved for denoting extremely small amounts

- Time constant – it is a unit of measurement that describes the output of a circuit's minimum or maximum output value; in a way, it refers to the measurement of time reaction

- Watt-hour – it is the unit of measurement that describes the electrical energy consumption over a period of time

IV.C. – Units of Force

Since *force* in a circuit is an important concept, it is advised that the particular unit of measurement is presented correctly. Even in physics, it is reiterated that it should be labeled according to its right category.

Atomic and electrostatic units of force:

- Hartrees

- Newtons

- Tesla

- Coulombs

- Meters

Chapter V – Power Transfer at Max

There will be instances of a *power transfer* in a circuit. For the electricity to continue its smooth flow, its original energy source will be replaced with an internal energy source. With such a change (especially in the case of a series circuit where power needs to flow continuously), the explanation for its system's pattern becomes a notch challenging.

For *beginners*, a great way of understanding *power transfer* in a circuit is to understand maximum power transfer, along with the concepts that dwell on the topic. As it follows, by gaining clarity on how much was the original power, as well as how much power a particular circuit can handle, you can see whether a power transfer is necessary or will only cause its load to be compromised.

V.A. – Maximum Power Transfer

Maximum power transfer, a concept that was introduced by Moritz von Jacobi sometime in the 1840s, draws light on the idea that for maximum external power to be obtained, an internal resistance needs to be in place. However, the transfer can only be flawless if the original resistance is equal to the potential power that an internal resistor can produce.

Consequently, maximum power transfer yields results that point out *power transfer*, and not *efficiency*; while improved efficiency can be a byproduct, it is not the chief purpose of maximum power transfer. It implies that although higher percentage of power is transferrable, it does not affect the magnitude of the power load (i.e. the extent that it can affect a circuit). In the event that the internal resistance is modified to accommodate a value higher than the value of the original resistance, improved efficiency can be achieved.

Moreover, the concept of maximum power transfer was initially misunderstood; a subject of many arguments was a circuit's reduced efficiency with the occurrence of transfer. Some insisted that due to the potential power that is lost during an exchange, a circuit may fail to reach 100% efficiency. As emphasis of this group's angle, take for example the case of a motor whose power is transferred from a battery; power in this situation may not be maximized, and it will only be realized over time when battery power has been fully consumed.

The maximum power theory states that the task of transferring power consumes power, too

It was *Thomas Edison*, as well as his fellow scientists, *Francis Robbins Upton*, who contested that maximum power transfer and efficiency are only *relative*; the 2 concepts are not one and the same. In fact, there is a discussion about *maximum power efficiency*, too.

In the exchange, you will find that *resistance* plays an important role. By giving light to the former argument, you can calculate a circuit's capability of a maximum power transfer, in relation to maximum power efficiency with the following formula:

$MPT = RL \div (RL + RS)$

A circuit's *MPT* (or maximum power transfer) can be determined with basic arithmetic skills. First, divide the *RL* (or Resistance Load) by the sum of the *RL* and *RS* (or Resistance Source).

V.B. – Thevenin's Theory

Thevenin's Theory, conceptualized by Hermann von Helmholtz and Leon Charles Thevenin, discusses that if a circuit follows a linear network, any point can be replaced given that it remains to carry a source for current, resistance, and voltage. Behind it, the idea is to supply an equivalent.

Originally, *Thevenin's Theory* can only be applied to circuits that operate with a DC system; since a DC system is rather simple, replacing its components with an equivalent is possible. Eventually, however, its capability to handle a load in a non-linear system was discovered; it can offer solutions for an AC system.

Moreover, the *Thevenin Theory* puts emphasis on that the average circuit can only be considered to have a linear according to a limited range; it can only be replaced by the components of with values among the range.

The Thevenin Theory follows that power dissipation can yield unique values, and can also yield identical values. However, the results can only be accomplished with the power supplied by an external resistor.

V.C. – The Star Delta Transformation

The *Star Delta Transformation* dwells on the idea that a circuit's system can change from one phase to another. For instance, if a circuit's power source is altered, its ability of carrying power from a point to the next is altered, too. Especially if there are 3 branches in a circuit's system, the power that circulates is known to form a closed loop.

The Star Delta Transformation refers to 2 kinds of circuit transformations. The first circuit transformation is a star transformation, which can be described by a "Y" formation; the second circuit transformation is a delta transformation, which can be described by a triangular pattern.

Moreover, the Star-Delta Transformation describes a 3-phase network of circuits, which can explain power transfer between these 3 networks. It enables the conversion of impedances that are connected to each other. With the theory as basis, alongside getting a clear scope for power transfer analysis, solving various concerns can be accomplished, too; the concept is applicable to different types of circuits including *series circuits, bridge-type networks, resistive circuits,* and *parallel circuits.*

The Star-Delta Transformation can be converted to the Delta-Star Transformation. From the star or Y-formation, the circuit creates a triangular network as the transition is achieved.

The Star-Delta Transformation or the Delta-Star Transformation is also called the Y-Δ Transformation or the Δ-Y Transformation

For the transition of the Star-Delta Transformation into the Delta-Star Transformation, a formula should be followed; this is meant to ensure that the transformation, along with the calculations for the total resistance in *all 3 circuits*, is successful. Initially, the goal is to compare the amount of power in an individual network. Once the power in network 1 has been acknowledged, proceed to identifying the weight that one network holds in the entire formation; one way of determining this is to disconnect that entire network and observe the operations of a circuit.

The formula:

**representations: $_\Delta R$ = total resistance of the transformation

$_1N$ = resistance in node 1

$_2N$ = resistance in node 2

$_AR$ = resistance in circuit A

$_BR$ = resistance in circuit B

$_CR$ = resistance in circuit C

$_\Delta R\,(_1N\,_2N) = {_C}R\,||\,(_AR + {_B}R)$

The simple version of the formula:

**representation: TR = total resistance

$_AR$ = resistance in circuit A

$_BR$ = resistance in circuit B

$_CR$ = resistance in circuit C

$_TR = {_A}R + {_B}R + {_C}R$

V.D. – Extra Element Theory

A circuit analysis technique that can be used for the simplification of a complicated problem is *the Extra Element Theory*; it was proposed by R.D. Middlebrook. The idea behind it is to take a complex matter, then divide it into small portions; each of the small portions will be addressed.

It follows that every circuit has a *transfer function* and *driving point*; the process of analyzing a circuit, therefore, can become easier if the aforementioned elements are first identified.

In the Extra Element Theory, unlike in other circuitry theorems, an element such as a capacitor or resistor can be temporarily removed so the transfer function or driving point can be determined. Since there are circuit components that can complicate an equation (regardless of how integral they are to a circuit), it is practical to set them aside for a while; although they may be of value to a circuit as a whole, it was proven that they don't affect calculations. Once the initial goal is achieved, the elements can be returned.

Impedance is a familiar term in discussions of the Extra Element Theory; it can be analyzed with the employment of the theory. In certain cases, its input can be determined in network granted that an *extra element* joins in.

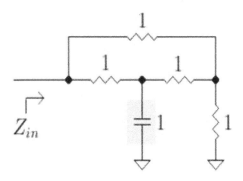

The Extra Element Theory (in relation to input impedance) proposes the addition of an "extra" element that is equivalent in value to the other elements

The formula for finding the impedance is:

**representations: Z = impedance

s = source

Z = 1 ÷ s

V.E. – Simplification of the Source

Simplification of the Source, sometimes referred to as Source Transformation, is the process of converting electric current into voltage, or voltage into electric current. It is a common technique used by many circuit engineers for explaining their circuit's system in simple terms.

The process of Simplification of the Source usually begins with an existing resistance source in a circuit; it is then replaced with new electric current source with a similar level of resistance. Since it is *bilateral procedure*, one can be derived to yield results from another. It makes way for the adjustment of voltage as it gradually becomes the equivalent of a particular circuit's resistance.

Moreover, *Simplification of the Source* may begin with an existing resistance, but is *not limited to the accommodation of resistive circuits*. It means that the process can be performed on circuits that involve inductors and capacitors.

V.F. – Where Does the Rosenstark Method Fit in?

The *Rosenstark Method*, sometimes called *Asymptotic Gain Model*, is yet another important subject where power transfer is concerned. In light of the return ratio, it serves as the representation of *negative gain* from feedback amplifiers. As it provides an intuitive form of circuit analysis, it introduces a new batch of elements such as the *return ratio* and *asymptotic gains*.

The Rosenstark formula:

**representations: G_o = 0 asymptotic gain

G_∞ = infinite asymptotic gain

T = return ratio

Rosenstark Method = $\{G_o + [T \div (T + 1)]\} + \{G_\infty + [T \div (T + 1)]\}$

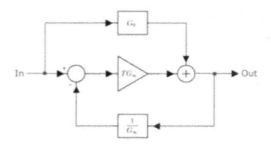

Circuit Engineering: The Beginner's Guide to Electronic Circuits, Semi-Conductors, Circuit Boards and Basic Electronics

The Rosenstark Method serves as the basic representation of power transfer in a circuit

Best features of the Rosenstark Method:

- Assumes that the direct transmission is small and can be equated to the asymptotic gain

- Characterizes bilateral properties and feedback amplifiers

- Identifies (via thorough inspection) the passive circuit elements

Steps:

1. Choose a source in a circuit's system; preferably, opt for a dependent source.

2. Determine the source's return ratio.

3. Identify the G_∞.

4. Identify the G_O.

5. Use the Rosenstark formula and substitute values.

Chapter VI – Laws, Laws & More Laws

Come to think of it, *circuit analysis* is one of the broad branches of electrical engineering. It covers the basics of circuits and power consumption; it also covers the extensive aspects of the topic such as the operations of an entire electrical network.

Without laws regarding how electric current is distributed within a circuit's components, there is a risk of unclear discussions of *fundamental and in-depth analysis*; without them, a guide that can break down lengthy components is absent. For beginners, especially, they are important since they grant the chance to understand the functions of a circuit and even each one of its parts. It stays true to the idea that for the resolution of a big problem, looking at it like little pieces is an opportunity to conqueror its difficulties.

VI.A. – Putting Kirchhoff's Laws into Motion

Kirchhoff's Laws are composed of *2 equations* that dwell on the conservation of charge and energy. They were initially introduced in 1845 by Gustav Kirchhoff as a means for the determination of a circuit's power consumption, as well as its parameters.

As several discussions go, Kirchhoff's Laws may not be too important since it was derived from the work of Scottish physicist, *James Maxwell*; since it was derived from another's work, it is said that a circuit engineer should rather use the original work as basis. However, it is a set of laws that primarily focuses on the operations of a closed circuit; the previous work from which it was taken doesn't put emphasis on a closed circuit, and is rather descriptive of the generic circuit.

Moreover, Kirchoff's Laws are conditional. It may be useful in describing charge and energy conservation for different circuit elements, but it can only yield an *approximation*; it also requires certain factors such as changing electric currents, voltage, and resistance.

Kirchhoff's Law is actually a general term. To be specific, it addresses 2 subjects: current and voltage. It acknowledges all circuits, regardless of complexities.

To solidify its argument in the conservation of charge and energy, one of Kirchhoff's Laws, *KCL* (or Kirchhoff's Current Law), states that the electric current in an interconnected network is relative. And, to emphasize his point, Gustav Kirchhoff contests that the algebraic sum of the electric current in a joint network is *0*.

Another law of Kirchhoff that complements the KCL is *KVL* (or Kirchhoff's Voltage Law). Its basis is on the general law on energy conservation that defines voltage as the energy per unit of charge. Just like in the previous law, Gustav Kirchhoff says that in a closed network, the algebraic sum of the electric voltage in a joint network is *0*.

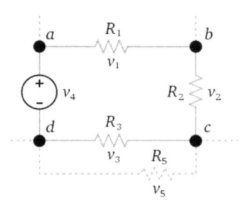

According to KVL, adding all the voltages within the circuit yields 0

VI.B. – Does Michael Faraday Know What He's Getting Into?

The *Law of Induction* by *Michael Faraday* is a fundamental law that revolves around the field of a circuit and the possible elements that are subject to eventual interaction. It carries both qualitative and quantitative aspects, and proposes that only with the presence of an infinite source of inductors can a circuit retain its inductive capability.

Unfortunately, not all circuit engineers and scientists are one with *Michael Faraday* and his *Law of Induction*. It is argued that although it holds some matters true, especially where loops of wire are concerned, it can yield the wrong results if used extensively; it can only handle a certain field and is usually arbitrarily small. In fact, counterexamples were previously presented.

A counterexample of Faraday's Law of Induction is the case involving an *electric disc generator*. Due to its own magnetic field, it can rotate circularly at a specified angular rate; it can complete a rotation and in the process, induct electricity by distributing it to other areas (within the circuit). It can be deduced that although the circuit's shape has remained constant over a period of time and although it can induct electricity, its distributive method made it lose inductive capabilities.

An electric disc generator induces electricity until cycle completion in the object's lower brush.

Faraday's Law of Induction may have been noted for certain flaws, but it is a law that made the conception of other important laws (not all of them are in the field of circuit engineering) possible. An important law with basis on Michael Faraday's idea is Albert Einstein's *Special Relativity*.

VI.C. - Ohm's Law & Conductivity

Ohm's Law, named after the German scientist, Georg Simon Ohm, is a powerful law that describes the resistance and electric current in a circuit, as well as their potential difference. Particularly, it sheds light on 2 points, then, subjects them to further analysis. Consequently, the relationship between Point A and Point B will indicate each of their properties as individual components.

In the verge of learning its concepts, it will dawn on you that *Ohm's Law* is an *empirical matter*. After observations with different ranges of length scales, it was proposed that it would fail where small wires are concerned; however, this proved to be a mere assumption since it was discovered that it could function regardless of a wire's size.

Since it is a basic equation in circuit engineering, *Ohm's Law* can also be applied for the determination of metal conductivity; it can be relied on when it comes to understanding the electric flow and conductive aspect in a circuit's component. Various materials that make use of Georg Ohm's principles are referred to as *ohmic*.

Georg Ohm set the parameters for his law to include only common terms in circuitry

In the physics of electricity, Ohm's Law is important where quantitative measurements in a circuit are concerned. Initially, when it was presented to German scientists, it was only mocked and rejected due to the mere fact that it went against the basic understanding of electric flow; it was dismissed as "a web of fancies" and worse, Georg Ohm was dubbed as a "fancy but invaluable" science professor. It was only until 1840 when it earned recognition and is now widely used today.

How to calculate for the elements in Ohm's Law:

Formula # 1:

voltage = current* resistance

Formula # 2:

current = voltage ÷ resistance

Formula # 3:

resistance = voltage ÷ current

VI.D. – The Argument of Norton's Theorem

Edward Lawry Norton, as he implies in *Norton's Theorem*, proposed that in circuit analysis, any linear network, granted that it has sources of voltage, electric current, and resistance, has an equivalent in dual network. A certain system may be unique, but values that can make a similar model can be obtained.

To find a circuit's equivalent using Norton's concepts, certain values need to be identified: voltage, electric current, and resistance. Once there are clear sources, you can begin formulating the necessary equations. However, when the sources are dependent on each other, another (and it has to be from a generic source) electric current needs to enter the picture.

Moreover, Norton's Theorem gives light to the fact that the values for the *equivalent current* and *equivalent voltage* are values that can be identified at the first 2 terminals of a circuit. It is important to note, however, that such a case is only possible if all the components in the said circuit are *short-circuited*. If the components are not short-circuited, a practical solution is to have current and voltage sources replaced; current can be replaced by transforming a circuit into an open circuit, and voltage can be replaced by transforming a circuit into a short circuit.

Norton's Theorem was also developed by Hands Ferdinand Mayer

The formula:

**representations: TC_{AB} = total current in circuit A and circuit B

TC = total current

34

TC_{AB} = voltage ÷ (TC in circuit A + TC in circuit B)

VI.E. – Coulomb's Law

One of the laws that underwent heavy testing is a law that gives importance to the electrostatic relationship of all the charged elements within a circuit; this law is called *Coulomb's Law* after the scientist, Charles Agustin de Coulomb. It argues that the magnitude of interactive circuit components is in direct proportion to the *squared area* between the distances. To demonstrate a point, it shows that the primary force works along a straight line.

Moreover, Coulomb's Law requires that the placement of the charged elements is accomplished through a single medium. This causes the arrangement to eliminate any possible complications.

The application of Coulomb's Law is only valid if the circuit components are point charges

To make it effortless to obey Coulomb's Law, the determination of *Coulomb's constant* is recommended. Once the value of the constant has been determined, not only is it easier to adhere to the aforementioned law, you are also ensuring that the calculations for the electric current are valid.

The formula:

**representations: CC = Coulomb's Constant

ε_o = electric constant

$CC = 1 ÷ 4\pi \times \varepsilon_o$

Chapter VII – Understanding Electromagnetism

A pair of loudspeakers is an example of an electronic device that works due to the *strategic positioning* of circuit elements. That, along with the integral parts called *electromagnets*; such components cause disturbance to other circuit elements. Their effect on their fellows is rather significant as they tend to make the device's cone to vibrate. As a result, sound, and in most cases, high quality sound, is produced.

For a deeper understanding of a loudspeaker, you could use a lesson in *electromagnetism.*

VII.A. – An Introduction to the Concept behind Electromagnetism

Electromagnetism is a branch of science that involves the study of electricity and magnetism. It follows that wherever there is an electric field, there is also a magnetic field. It was initially introduced and developed by *Hans Christian Orsted.* In 1802, an Italian scholar by the name of *Gian Domenico Romagnosi* also examined the field

In circuitry, understanding the concept behind electromagnetism is important due the possibly strong electromagnetic reaction of circuit components. It follows that the *EMF* (or electromagnetic force) of any circuit serves a major role in the determination of internal properties.

Chapter V, *Power Transfer at Max,* and Chapter VI, *Laws, Laws & More Laws,* contain different discussions about transferring electric current and voltage. In electromagnetism, more discussions about transfer will be tackled. This time, however, the focus is on the charged elements in a circuit (whether negatively or positively charged), as well as their responses when exposed to movement.

The primary principles of electromagnetism:

- The direction of a magnetic field dictates the direction of the current in a circuit

- The electric current of a conductor creates a magnetic field; the formation is dependent on the direction of the conductor, but is always shaped in a corresponding circle

- The magnetic poles of charged elements always come in pairs; one pole in a pair needs to be inversely proportional to the other

- Charged elements can either attract or repel; elements with different charges are attractive to each other, while those with similar charges avoid contact

- Electric current can be induced when it is moved away or toward a magnetic field

VII.B. – Gauss Who?

A notable individual in the field of electromagnetism is *Carl Friedrich Gauss*. He is a German mathematician who put together the critical electromagnetism concepts in the form of a law called *Gauss Law*. According to him, to determine the relevance of the distribution of electric charges, the circuit's electric field, in its entirety, must be evaluated.

Gauss Law allows mathematical expression with the employment of *integral* and *differential calculus*, preferably in vector form. For a beginner in circuitry, the particular technique of demonstration is advised since it grants a clear perspective of the concept of electromagnetism.

The integral formula:

**representations: Φ_E = electric field

ε_0 = electric constant

Q = total electric charge

$\Phi_E = Q \div \varepsilon_0$

The differential formula:

**representations: ∇ = an electric field's divergence

E = the other half of an electric field's divergence

p = electric charge density

ε_0 = electric constant

$\nabla \times E = p \div \varepsilon_0$

VII.C. – The Main Formulas in Electromagnetism

In a circuit's electromagnetic field, it is important to remember that charged elements tend to move radically; sometimes, predicting the direction of the electric flow is nearly impossible. While others go about in a non-linear network, many charges obey the rule of superposition since they adhere to a linear path. With the use of certain laws as basis, the relationship between the charged elements can be evaluated.

4 laws:

1. Ampere's Law – an important law whose applications include instances of a moving magnetic field; particularly, it be applied in situations involving current-carrying wires

   The formula:

   **representations: B = electromagnetic field

   DL = differential element of the electric current

   μo = permeability of o space

   I = electric current in an enclosed circuit

   $\int B \times DL = \mu o \times I$

2. Biot-Savart's Law – a law that is employed for the calculation of steady current in an electromagnetic field; a requirement is a constant time variable, as well as a charge that is a subject of neither a build-up or depletion

   The formula:

   **representations: B = electromagnetic field outside a circuit

   μo = permeability of o space

   I = electric current in an enclosed circuit

   R = distance from the electromagnetic field

   $B = \int (\mu o \times I) \div 4\pi R^2$

3. Faraday's Law – like his [Michael Faraday] law of induction, this is a law that addresses the induced electromagnetic force of an object; it is strictly applicable to the charged elements within a closed circuit

   The formula:

   **representations: IEMF = induced electromagnetic field

   Dφ = difference of space

   DT = time differential

   $IEMF = - D\varphi \div DT$

4. Lorentz Force – a law that assesses a point charge due to both an electromagnetic field and an electric field

   The formula:

**representations: LF = Lorentz Force

q = total charge

EMF = electromagnetic field inside a circuit

V = velocity

B = electromagnetic field outside a circuit

$$LF = q\,[EMF + (V \times B)]$$

VII.D. – Electrodynamics & Quantum Electrodynamics

Before the 1900s, a scientist named William Gilbert addressed a proposal concerning *electricity* and *magnetism*; according to him, while both subjects can be traced to attracting and repulsing objects within a circuit, electricity and magnetism are different concepts. The key to understanding electromagnetism, therefore, is to understand the individual terms; particularly, understand their relevance and distinction.

A conflict regarding electromagnetism is that, despite agreeing to Albert Einstein's *Special Relativity*, it goes against some of the rules of mechanics; it is only dependent on the electromagnetic permeability of o space. It follows that in the case of moving frames, the electromagnetic field is subjected to transformation to include space.

Moreover, all electromagnetic phenomena are covered under *quantum mechanics*. This makes the electromagnetic field of a circuit accountable for the physical phenomena that are observable, especially *magnetism* and *electricity*.

Chapter VIII – Let's Talk Circuit Boards

Are you familiar with *crocodile clips*?

Crocodile clips are devices that can be used for the assembly of a circuit; these tools are so-named for their resemblance to the jaws of a crocodile. With them, a solid grip to connect a component is possible. If you're wondering how electrical engineers can create electrical connections without the associated dangers? Well, there's your answer.

By using *crocodile clips*, you can make a model of a working circuit. Whether be it a basic circuit, a series circuit, or a parallel circuit, you can create for an audience to analyze.

VIII.A. - Printed Circuit Boards 101

Printed circuit boards (or PCBs) are devices that enable electrical connectivity even in an "open" environment; within their system, there are resistors, inductors, transformers, capacitors, conductors, and semi-conductors. These tools support high component density. In a way, printed circuit boards are referred to as *live circuits*.

Since functioning circuit boards can be rather risky, especially when exposed to extreme environments, they are packaged accordingly. In most cases, these devices are subjected to a series of coating procedures and are dipped in acrylic, wax, polyurethane, and epoxy.

Design standards:

- Templates and card dimensions are designed according to required circuitry regulations
- Manufactured Gerber data are generated
- Design is planned thoroughly with the assistance of an *EDA or Electronic Design Automation* tool
- Traces for signals are routed
- Copper thickness and layer thickness are carefully evaluated

VIII.B. – Circuit Board Tests

To see if a circuit works, certain tests are performed. Particularly, it is determined whether or not it is functional and can perform desired tasks. Along with its capacitors, resistors, transformers, and other components, it is analyzed for opens and shorts.

Objectives of testing methods:

- To detect flaws
- To detect error-free operations of each of its components
- To determine system stability
- To evaluate whether it is fit for use
- To evaluate safety issues
- To verify test systems

Example testing methods:

- Analog tests
- Contact tests
- Contact tests
- Electrolytic capacitor tests
- Flash tests
- Powered digital tests
- Short tests

VIII.C. – Let's Learn to Prototype

Prototyping is the ability to put a particular idea to test by preparing a model from which other circuits are developed. Especially when the circuit in subject involves a complex system or expensive components, a prototype is initially designed.

If the circuit creator is unsure of how a particular circuit will function, his best bet is to create a *prototype*. This way, he can evaluate his creation and see how it can be improved. If it's not yielding his desired results, he can modify the placements of each of its components until he achieves a necessary output. Otherwise, he can proceed to the actual circuit-making process.

VIII.D. - The Art of Bread-Boarding

Breadboards allow the creation of a circuit prototype, which is the reason why these tools are ideal for beginners. *Bread-boarding*, therefore, is the process of creating a circuit prototype in a board to resemble the operations of a real circuit. Its history can be traced to the time that electrical enthusiasts would use a literal breadboard (i.e. the board used for slicing bread).

According to experts, it's recommended to learn and understand bread-boarding prior to making your first-ever circuit. It's advised to be familiar with each of its components, as well as how it works.

Breadboard components:

- Chips – these are *legs* that come out of both sides of a breadboards; these components fit perfectly and serve as connectors of different parts

- Posts – these are components that enable connections from power sources

- Power rails – these are vertical metal rows strips that are adjacent to terminals; through these components, easy access to a power source can be provided

- Power supplies – these are components that enable the supplementation of a wide range of electric current and voltage levels

- Terminals – these are horizontal metal row strips that are adjacent to power rails; through these components, wires are allowed to be inserted, then, be held intact

VIII.E. – Essential Skills in Circuitry

After understanding *bread-boarding*, you're almost ready for some hands-on circuit lessons. First, however, you should adopt a certain set of skills; while bread-boarding is helpful, it's only practice (i.e. for instance, there is no soldering involved). Since you'll be making an actual functioning circuit, it's time to get your hands dirty.

5 skills required in circuitry:

1. Stripping (wire) – it is a skill that promotes secure electrical connections; it involves the knowledge on various types of wires, thickness of wires, and how to maintain a solid grip; since exposure to electric current is a risk, it is best to check out the appropriate tools for wires

2. Drilling – it is a skill that focuses on the proper drilling (of holes) in a circuit, then, making sure that electrical connections can remain intact; it is a slow process that requires practice with accuracy and precision

3. How to test batteries – it is a skill that requires testing the capacity of a battery; particularly, it involves measuring the current load in open and short circuits

4. How to use a glue gun – it is a skill that takes advantage of a glue gun's conductive property; it teaches how to insulate and how to set a semi-permanent coating; especially when there is a need to strengthen the joints of a circuit, it comes in handy

5. How to use liquid electrical coating – it is a skill that focuses on the ability to apply liquid electrical coating where conventional electrical tape is likely to fail; it requires precaution since about 30% of the parts in the liquid coating are quite volatile

VIII.F. – The Secrets of a Solder

Soldering is a process that involves (at least) 2 metals (or any conductive material); the 2 metals are joined by flowing and melting. In the industry of circuitry, it is one of the most fundamental methods in circuit creation; it allows independent components to work as one.

A technique of good soldering revolves around the knowledge of the amount of heat that is applied. For *basic soldering*, *361F* is the temperature to consider and for *advanced soldering*, the goal is to arrive at a temperature of somewhere between *361F to 419F*.

In *metallurgical engineering*, a term named *flux* is commonly used; in circuit engineering, as soon as the circuit creation process commences, it will be introduced, too. It is cleaning agent and a flowing material that facilitates the soldering process. Should there be invisible impurities (e.g. oil, dirt, etc.), they will be removed for the purpose of not risking the integrity of a circuit.

Moreover, it is important to note that in soldering, the proper application of flux is suggested. Improper methods can result to joint failure. The system's damage (due to incorrect flux application) may not be obvious at first, but gradually, it is capable of corrosion and rendering a circuit useless.

Chapter IX – Sufficient Safety

On a sunny day, try heading outside of your house, then, checking out the electrical connections (wires) from one post to another. More likely, one, two, or even a flock of birds are calmly resting on power lines.

Do you ever wonder why they don't get shocked?

No, birds are normal creatures; they do not possess extra-special powers. In their heads, they understand that it's a must not to step on open electrical networks, which is one of the things that need to be covered for beginners in circuit engineering.

IX.A. – The Lack of Electrical Safety Courses

While some *circuit engineering professors* teach enough lessons about *electrical safety*, others are quite behind on the area. They assume that practical knowledge, as well as a general "be careful" would suffice; since the beginners in circuit engineering are frequent exposure to electrical devices, no, the statement won't cut it. Therefore, it is important to stress out the need to be careful especially during their first hands-on activity.

Electrical safety tips:

- Treat each electrical device as if live current is running inside it (regardless if you're aware that there isn't)

- Overloading sockets for a circuit board? Not a good idea

- To cut off running current, add a residual current

- Always disconnect (and not just turn off) electrical devices when working on a component

- Always turn off any electrical device if not in use

- Regularly check the conditions of sockets and plugs

- Practice extreme caution when dealing with liquids and electric current

- Make sure your hands are dry

- Avoid octopus connections (i.e. devices that enable multiple plugs or sockets)

- Keep electrical wires and cords tucked neatly

- Wear the proper attire when creating a circuit; put on non-conductive gloves and footwear with insulated soles

IX.B. - The Importance of Hands-on Circuit Lessons

Hands-on learning is important for a beginner in circuits. It gives light to the fact that in circuit engineering, it is more about actual field work. Once the concepts are understood, it's best to move on to creating functional circuit boards.

A common problem that is encountered by beginners? Sweaty hands. Even in an air-conditioned laboratory, there are people who have to deal with sweaty hands when handling circuits. Alongside, they have to deal with the need of maintaining a strong and solid grip on various tools. Although this may be a concern, it's one that requires practice.

IX.C. – The 80-20 Rule of Circuit Safety

In circuitry, there is a rule that focuses on the installments of transmitters in hazardous areas for devices with a circuit; it is called the *80-20 Rule of Circuit Safety*. According to the rule, it is recommended to take extra precaution when dealing with particular portions of an electronic device; there are some parts that increase the risk of electrical shock when *touched* or *moved*.

Hazardous areas of a circuit (that require extra precaution):

- Point with high impedance

- Point with high resistance

- Area near the voltage source

- Area near an opening

- Area with conductive elements

IX.D. – Troubleshooting Concerns

In the event that a device with a circuit is not function correctly, it is recommended to have it evaluated accordingly. While a beginner may handle the task of checking, a professional in circuitry is the one who is advised to assess the system. Since an expert is already familiar with different circuit components, and he knows exactly where to look for possible faults, he is more qualified for the job.

Troubleshooting tips:

- Determine whether the connections are secure

- Determine whether the wires are correctly connected to one another

- Check for circuit components that seem out of place

- Check for circuit components that may be larger in size

Chapter X – Here's a Multimeter for You!

An important and indispensible tool in circuitry is a *multimeter*.

Imagine a situation when a circuit project was presented to you. Since you were requested to detail accurate measurements for its electric current, voltage, and resistance, you go to the nearest equipment laboratory to borrow a stack of devices for assistance.

Now, imagine the same situation, but this time, you have this tool; instead of having to go to the equipment laboratory to borrow a stack of devices to measure the electric current, voltage, and resistance, you turn to that tool. This particular time, you have a multimeter.

If you're not familiar with the operations of a multimeter, let it be your first job prior to creating a circuit project. It's actually quite easy to use. So long as you are attentive to instructions, and you know its components, certain restriction, and the technique to maximizing its functions, you're set.

X.A. - What's a Multimeter?

A multimeter, also called a multitester, *Volt-Ohm millimeter*, and *Volt-Ohm meter*, is an electronic device that measures the electric current in a circuit; it is capable of measuring voltage, resistance, and a variety of other units in a circuit's system. To know how to use the device, it's important to be familiar with each of its components; if you can understand how the components work, you can also understand the operations of the entire device.

Parts of a multimeter:

1. The selection knob – it enables a user to choose a particular setting that is subject for measurement

2. The display meter – it enables the display of the measured reading; it can contain up to 4 digits, as well as a negative sign

3. The probes – these are plugged into a multimeter that can interpret and convert measurements from a device into a multimeter; usually, these come in a pair of red and black probes

    Types of probes:

    I.   IC hook

    II.   Alligator clips

    III.   Test probes

X.B. - A Multimeter in the Works

Inarguably, a multimeter is one of the most useful tools in circuitry and one of the tools that can make the task of building circuits easy. It can be used to measure *any object or device* that contains a circuit and an electric current. Using it, however, comes the hard part; in fact, in the world of circuits and electronics, it earned the title as one of the most challenging jobs. It may be effortless to get a reading, but getting an accurate reading, then interpreting the reading is another story.

How to use a multimeter to measure (a basic example):

1. Prepare an AAA battery.

2. Plug the black probe of a multimeter to the negative side (i.e. the side with a "-") of the AAA battery.

3. Plug the red probe of a multimeter to the positive side of the AAA battery.

4. Check the display meter; as recommended, check the meter twice.

5. List down the reading and begin the interpretation.

X.C. – Resolution, Accuracy & Input Impedance

The smallest part of a multimeter's scale is called as the *resolution*. It is responsible for achieving an accurate reading and interpretation. In many multimeter kinds, especially digital ones, it can be configured or *calibrated*. And, as the rules go, a device with low resolution doesn't require much completion time; a device with high resolution can require a demanding processing time.

Meanwhile, the *accuracy* of a multimeter refers to an error in the measurement of an electric current, in comparison to a perfect reading. It is relative to the device's resolution since resolution may not be calibrated accordingly if the absolute accuracy level is questionable. Therefore, to determine the total accuracy of a multimeter, its relative accuracy should be added to its absolute accuracy.

Formula for the computation of total accuracy:

**representations: TA = total accuracy

RA = relative accuracy

AA = absolute accuracy

$TA = RA + AA$

When talking about a multimeter's resolution and accuracy, *input impedance* is a set of terms that needs to be acknowledged, too. This is due to the device's inability to achieve accurate readings when it is not set accordingly. Especially for the measurement of a circuit's voltage, its input impedance has to be calibrated high (i.e. higher than a circuit's voltage) so the operation remains smoothly.

X.D. – Safety Concerns

Groups that are in charge of the manufacture of multimeters, as well as the authorities that promote the safe use of such devices have set safety standards. This is to emphasize the importance of the right employment of the electrical tools. Although the method for use can be rather straightforward, reckless habits can result to problems. Alongside the possibility of inaccurate readings, it can cause harm to the individual that is handling the devices.

Categories of safety standards:

- Category 1 – applicable to the employment of a multimeter, circuit, or any electronic equipment with a distance near main connections

- Category 2 – applicable to the employment of a multimeter, circuit, or any electronic equipment with a distance somewhere near the first phase of main connections

- Category 3 –applicable to the employment of a multimeter, circuit, or any electronic equipment with a distance near permanently installed loads

- Category 4 – applicable to the employment of a multimeter, circuit, or any electronic equipment with a distance near faulty current levels that can be quite high

Chapter XI - DIY Circuits: Simple Projects

When you're into circuits, as well as *electronics and electrical engineering*, you need to step up your game when it comes to building items. Isn't the main reason for learning the branch of electrical engineering for the creation of circuits, then, putting them to good use?

In the event that your first circuit project wouldn't turn out as desired, try not to get discouraged easily, and instead, give matters another go. Not getting the results you wanted maybe a bit of a downer, but eventually, the odds will be in your favor; look at the setback as an opportunity for learning. If your heart's into circuits, you'll soon get the hang of how things are done.

XI.A. – Common Tools in Circuitry

For the creation of a circuit, you can make use of just about any tool you come across; if you find equipment that will make you accomplish a task easier, then, maybe you should put it in your arsenal. You *can* use just any tool, yes, but, doing so is not advised. It is best to choose the right set (i.e. a set of tools with a non-conductive handle) to not put your safety at risk.

Common tools:

- Crimper
- Cutters (e.g. cable cutter, electrical cutter, etc.)
- Extraction tool
- Glue gun
- Non-metallic tweezers
- Pliers
- Screwdriver
- Soldering gun
- Wire-wrapping tools

XI.B. - Beginner Circuit Projects

Building your first circuit can be a challenge; since you're still a beginner, you may end up making mistakes. Maybe your circuit won't end up as functional as desired, despite having followed your understanding of a series of procedures. In such a case, this is where you have to tweak your work; be diligent in figuring out where you went wrong. If you're uncertain of your actions' impact, don't worry too much. The important part is to begin; you can, then, figure out the rest along the way.

7 easy circuit projects (derived from http://www.instructables.com):

- Project # 1 – Static Electricity Analyzer

    The Static Electricity Analyzer can detect nearby static electricity; to indicate that static electricity is present, its LED component glows. Apart from a detector, it can be used to analyze the electricity in its surroundings. It is an extremely sensitive device since it can even detect nearby hand movement without touching the antenna.

Materials:

- Around 10 pieces wire

- 1 piece LED

- 1 piece static electricity antenna

- 1 piece 100K resistor

- 1 piece 1M resistor

- 3 pieces 2n222 transistor

Procedures (as shown in the layout above):

1. To the left side of the circuit board, connect the 1M resistor to 2n222 transistor.

2. Beside it, attach the wire, then, attach the static electricity antenna.

3. On the bottom, attach the wire, then, attach the other 2n222 transistor; next to it, attach the wire, and finally, attach the third 2n222 transistor.

4. Place the 100K resistor adjacent to the second 2n222 transistor.

5. Place the LED adjacent to the third 2n222 resistor.

6. Establish connection to a power supply.

- Project # 2 – Dark LED Light

The Dark LED Light is a circuit project that can detect darkness. It follows that when insufficient light is supplied, an IC timer is alerted; consequently, a high output is produced and LED light will be switched on. The idea behind it is similar to that of a street light that automatically turns on once it detects that it's already evening.

Materials:

- Around 10 pieces wire

- 1 piece LED

- 1 piece LDR

- 1 piece 10nf capacitor

- 1 piece 100nf capacitor

- 1 piece 10K resistor

- 1 piece 100K resistor

- 1 piece 555 IC timer

Procedures (as shown in the layout above):

1. On top of the LDR, attach the 100K resistor.

2. On the bottom of the LDR, create a connection to the LED.

3. To the left of the LED, create a connection to the 10nf capacitor.

4. To the left of the 10nf capacitor, create a connection to the 100nf capacitor.

5. Next to the 100nf capacitor, create a connection to the 10K resistor.

6. Place the 555 IC timer between all the connections; establish the main connection by attaching the other ends of the LED, LDR, capacitors, and resistors to the 555 IC timer (directly or with a wire).

7. Establish connection to a power supply.

- Project # 3 – The Ticking Bomb

The Ticking Bomb is meant for creating a ticking sound that resembles a bomb. Once it is turned on, it produces sound that is adjustable, but is modified to 1 tick per second.

Materials:

- Around 10 pieces wire
- 2 pieces 10uf capacitors
- 1 piece 555 IC timer
- 1 piece 47K resistor
- 1 piece 8 ohm speaker

Procedures (as shown in the layout above):

1. Make the 555 IC timer as the central component; to its left, create a connection to the 47K resistor.

2. On the bottom, create a connection to the first 10uf capacitor; then, create a connection from the 10uf capacitor to the 47K resistor.

3. To the right of the 555 IC timer, create a connection to the second 10uf capacitor.

4. From the second 10uf capacitor, create a connection to the 8 ohm speaker.

5. Establish connection to a power supply.

- Project # 4 – The Remote Tester

The Remote Tester, as its name suggests, is a circuit that checks whether or not a remote control is working. Behind it, the idea is focused on the sufficient amount of signals that the IR receiver is getting. If it receives enough signals, the LED lights up, which means that a particular remote control is functioning; conversely, if the LED remains as is, it is an indication of a faulty component in the device.

Materials:

- Around 10 pieces wire

- 1 piece LED

- 1 piece IR receiver

- 1 piece 1K resistor

- 1 piece bc557 transistor

- 1 piece 10uf capacitor

Procedures (as shown in the layout above):

1. On top of the bc557 transistor, create a connection to the LED.

2. Adjacent of the bc557 transistor (to the left), create a direct path to the 1K resistor, then, to the IR receiver.

3. On the bottom, create a connection to the 10uf capacitor.

4. Connect the 10uf capacitor (directly or with wire) to close the connection.

5. Establish connection to a power supply.

- Project # 5 – The Bell Experiment

    The Bell Experiment is a basic project that produces a musical sound; the result is a device that may be similar to a doorbell. It works according to each of its components; if the resistor, transistor, and IC are triggered, the bunch sends a signal to the speaker, which will then, create the sound.

Materials:

- Around 10 pieces wire

- 1 piece 1K resistor

- 1 piece 2n222 transistor

- 1 piece UM66 IC

- 1 piece 8 ohm speaker

Procedures (as shown in the layout above):

1. On one end of the 8 ohm speaker, create a connection to the 2n222 transistor.

2. On another end, create a connection to the 1K resistor.

3. From the 1K resistor, create a connection to the UM66 IC; make sure that the UM66 is parallel to the 8 ohm speaker.

4. Connect the UM66 (directly or with wire) to the 2n222 transistor to close the circuit.

5. Establish connection to a power supply.

- Project # 6 – The LED That Fades

The LED That Fades is a project that produces and sometimes, blinking lights. It operates according to the weakness or strength of the signals that are interpreted by each of its components. If its IC timer, transistor, resistor, and capacitor receive strong signals; the LED will glow; conversely, if they receive weak signals, the light starts to fade. In the event that the signals that are submitted are unstable (i.e. they alternate between weak or strong in a few minutes' time), the blinking pattern comes in.

Materials:

- Around 10 pieces wire
- 1 piece LED
- 1 piece 555 IC timer
- 1 piece bc547 transistor
- 1 piece 33K resistor
- 1 piece 220 ohm resistor
- 1 piece 100uf capacitor

Procedures (as shown in the layout above):

1. To the bottom of the bc547 transistor, create a connection to the LED.

2. Parallel to the LED, create a connection to the 100uf capacitor.

3. On top of the 100uf 33K resistor, create a connection to the 220 ohm resistor.

4. Next to the 220 ohm resistor, create a connection to the 555 IC timer.

5. Create a connection around the 555 IC timer for a closed circuit.

6. Establish connection to a power supply.

- Project # 7 – The LED with Activated Light

The LED with Activated Light is a basic project for beginners in circuit engineering; it is meant for a clearer understanding of the concept of resistance. The LED lights up with the application of sufficient resistance; if resistance levels are insufficient, the light won't be activated.

Materials:

- Around 10 pieces wire
- 1 piece LED
- 1 piece LDR
- 1 piece 10nf capacitor
- 1 piece 100nf capacitor
- 1 piece 10K resistor
- 1 piece 4.7K resistor
- 1 piece 555 IC timer
- 1 piece 220 ohm resistor

Procedures (as shown in the layout above):

1. To the bottom of the LDR, create a connection to the 4.7K resistor.

2. Parallel to the 4.7K resistor connection, create a new connection to the LED, followed by the 22 ohm resistor on top.

3. From the 22 ohm resistor, create a connection to the 555 IC timer.

4. To the bottom of the 555 IC timer, and parallel to the LED connection, create a new connection to the 10nf capacitor.

5. To the left of the 10nf capacitor, create a connection to the 100nf capacitor.

6. On top of the 100nf capacitor, create a connection to the 10K resistor.

7. Create a connection to close the circuit.

8. Establish connection to a power supply.

Chapter XII – Making Your Way to Circuit Design: PCB Layouts & Schematic Diagrams

If you are familiar with each of its components, you may have a good grasp of how an electronic circuit works; granted that the integral parts (e.g. power source, conductor, resistor, diode, etc.) are in place, and you were introduced to different techniques on establishing connections properly, there's a high chance that any circuit project you take on can be a success. Once an opening for a power source is identified, and the stability of an arrangement for the rest in a series is achieved, you're set.

However, if given the opportunity to make a particular circuit more functional, wouldn't you take it? Instead of settling for a random circuit design, why not have it modified for superior performance?

XII.A. - Circuit Design 101

Ever wonder why circuit engineers are paid highly and (depending on their chosen career path) are presented different career advancement opportunities (e.g. work as computer engineers, robotics specialists jobs, etc.)?

The responsibilities of circuit engineers are rather demanding; they need to be mentally tough and be open to different challenges. They spend hours and hours racking their brains out to determine how systems can be made more efficient. Chances are, there's always a way; it's up to them to look for one. When a particular project asks for it, it's mandatory for them to let their creative juices flow to arrive at a compatible solution. Otherwise, their built circuits may stop functioning eventually.

As mentioned, it's practical to design a circuit accordingly; especially with their employment for the fields of *communication, navigation, telecommunication, travel,* and other industries, their designs should consider a particular purpose. Apart from the objective of meeting different requirements, there needs to be a strategy since a more functional circuit comes with higher quality; it can make a project consume a reduced number of resources, too.

Reasons why there are various circuit designs:

- Improvement of a circuit's efficiency

- Improvement of a circuit's size and weight

- Guarantee a circuit's durability for a set period

- Guarantee a circuit is safe to use

XII.B. – The Design Process

Many times, a PCB layout (as discussed in chapter VII, *Let's Talk about Circuit Boards*) and a schematic diagram are often interchanged in circuitry; it has led others, especially the novices in circuit engineering, to believe that they are one and the same. In a way, since they are both presentations of a circuit's system, they may seem similar. However, upon closer inspection, they are not. It is, therefore, essential in the circuit design process that the difference is acknowledged.

A *PCB layout* is a physical representation or a *real model* of a circuit. It presents all of the electrical components that are included; it also details which of the components are active and which ones are passive. Although it can show an actual working circuit, understanding the functions of each of its parts can be tedious.

A PCB layout is an actual circuit model

On the other hand, a *schematic diagram*, also called simply as a circuit diagram, is a descriptive outline of a circuit's system; it is the standard and less costly way of circuit representation. It is like a PCB layout that shows both of the active and passive components in a circuit; unlike a PCB layout, however, its presentations can be easily understood.

Circuit Engineering: The Beginner's Guide to Electronic Circuits, Semi-Conductors, Circuit Boards and Basic Electronics

A schematic diagram can include important notes for the improvement of a circuit's design

Stages of circuit design:

- Meeting specific requirements

- The creation of a circuit diagram

- Building a breadboard, or a PCB layout

- The presentation of each circuit component (for professional evaluation)

- Applying the results of evaluation

- Testing (and retesting)

- Getting approval from professionals

Circuit design tips for beginners (preparation process):

- Categorize the components

- Construct a PCB layout, as well as a schematic diagram

- Determine the compatibility of each circuit component

Circuit design tips for beginners (circuit-building process):

- Always avoid cold solder joints

- Always separate power controls and other connections

- Always separate analog and digital components

- Create traces should hard-to-find components be included

- Remember to always make integral nodes accessible

- Solder the components systematically; solder small components first, then, solder larger components next

- Strategize the spaces you allow between components

- Take note of any heat spots

XII.C. - Circuit Symbols

On the process of building a circuit and modifying its design, an understanding of different circuit symbols is important. Descriptions of circuit components can be put in simple words; it is called a *verbal description*. However, since a thorough approach is recommended in many circuitry lessons, a visual representation can enable you to understand the electric flow in a circuit.

Here's a good comparison:

Verbal description	Visual representation
Circuit # 1 contains a light bulb, as well as D-cell battery as power source.	

Moreover, circuit symbols for a visual representation of a circuit is preferred over a verbal descriptions since they may be less complicated to understand. Especially if the particular circuit is quite advanced, a description containing words can be challenging to use as basis. If a visual model is employed, however, you can simply focus on connections, instead of the interpretation of a worded description; there is a better chance of building an impressive circuit design successfully. Especially if you have plans of advancing your place in circuit engineering by soon moving forward from a novice to a circuit expert, *memorizing* the different circuit symbols is a must.

List of basic symbols:

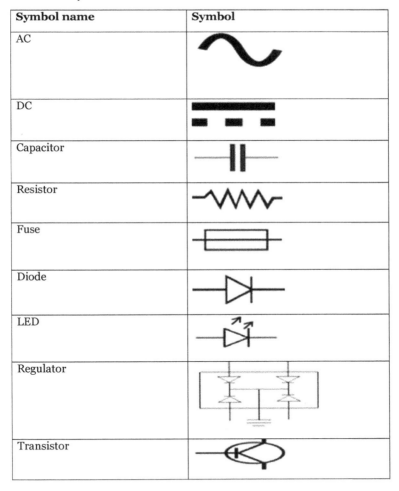

Symbol name	Symbol
AC	
DC	
Capacitor	
Resistor	
Fuse	
Diode	
LED	
Regulator	
Transistor	

List of basic capacitor variation symbols:

-

-

-

List of basic diode variation symbols:

-

Anode Cathode

-

Anode Cathode

-

Anode Cathode

-

List of basic switches variation symbols:

-

-

-

List of basic transistor variation symbols:

-

-

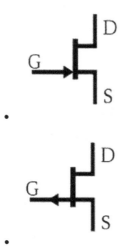

-

XII.D. – Factors to Consider

A strategic circuit design is important since a circuit may not function at all in the absence of a good plan; if the placement of each of its components wasn't accomplished according, you may have just wasted resources. You may have the correct components but if they are not designed properly, a circuit is far from working. Besides, at the realization that you may not be design a circuit's system according to requirements, you wouldn't want to put the circuit-building project to an end at the middle of the process, right?

Moreover, the proper design structure of a circuit needs to be prioritized. Regardless if it is not meant to impress another, it should still be designed accordingly as to be a stepping stone in the possibility of handling more projects eventually. With the knowledge of how to design a circuit properly as a beginner comes the effortless knowledge on the construction of more advanced circuits eventually.

What to keep in mind:

- Time availability (of the creator) – although it can be completed quickly, a circuit project shouldn't be rushed; the project creator should be available for a set period so he can concentrate properly on a circuit. Especially if he has hardly any time to spare, it's suggested that he either determines a way to find additional time, or takes on a different project

- Difficulty level – the assessment of a circuit project is important prior to acceptance. While there are simple ones, some projects are rather complicated. If a creator is certain that he can't follow through the procedures of a particular project, he may want to consider other undertakings

- Total cost of the project – one reason that the creation of a schematic diagram and other preparations are suggested (prior to taking on a circuit project) is due to practicality regarding the overall expenses. As much as possible, the creator should consider his ability to fund a project. Especially if he plans on using expensive circuit components, he needs to think about whether he can afford the project until completion.

- The desired function – identify the reason why you took on the project. Is it for experimentation and personal use? Or, was it a request from a company? Especially if the purpose is for a commercial company, design a circuit to achieve first-rate quality.

XII.E. - Documentation, Verification & Testing

A primary benefit of the *documentation* process is its advantage of letting you identify possible errors in putting together a circuit. If you weren't successful at the end stage of your project, you can figure out exactly where you went wrong; in favor of having to disregard your current progress and starting from scratch the second time around, you can simply have certain methods modified (for improvement).

Verification, as defined in circuitry, is the process of thoroughly evaluating each of a circuit's components, as well as each of the stages in the making. The objective is to determine whether the process has been adhered to correctly. Usually, this can be a time-consuming process, but since it is intend to ensure quality, it is an important one.

In a way, the real-world version of the verification process is *testing*. Prior to a circuit's launch and its exposure to different commercial industries, it is tested in research laboratories. Like verification, it can also be a time-consuming process, and since it is the last process before a circuit is passed on to another source, it can be a labor-intensive series.

Chapter XIII – A Way Is through EDA

Are you familiar with *FABS* or *Semi-conductor fabrication facilities?*

FABS are places where circuit designs, even complex ones, can be put together; they are usually extensive since they are meant to accommodate bulk circuit projects. Inside them are various equipment for *EDA*, which is why circuit-production is rapid.

With the productivity level of FABS, semi-conductors are continuously becoming popular. And, since semi-conductors are components in a circuit, circuits grew in popularity, too.

XIII.A. - What Is EDA?

EDA, also known as *Electronic Design Automation* is a class of software equipment especially for designing a circuit or different electronic devices. It is categorized along with other modern tools used in circuitry; it eliminates the need to design a circuit by hand, which minimizes simple and critical errors, repair glitches, and suggest possible improvements.

Moreover, it's due to EDA that circuit creation and circuit production became faster. If you're concerned regarding the quality since the process is done in an automated fashion, be confident that each design underwent thorough analysis. Remember, the software equipment's design was specifically meant to address a circuit's system.

XIII.B. – Design Flows

In the world of circuitry, it's important to be informed of the concepts of EDA; it privileges a circuit creator with a good grasp of the proper way to build circuits. The employees of grand electronics companies such as *Intel, Hewlett Packard*, and *Valid Logic Systems* are all trained to have impressive knowledge of the tools, despite already having gone through years of education.

Through the years, EDA tools have undergone continuous development. Initially, the concepts were rather limited; in the *Age of EDA Invention,* the focus was merely on *routing, logic synthesis, static analysis,* and *placement.* Eventually, in the *Age of EDA Implementation,* these concepts were subjected to major improvements; more *sophisticated and advanced algorithm* for the EDA tools were considered. Come the *Age of EDA Integration*, they were further studied and were designed to cater to integrated environments.

Now, you may be wondering why there is a need to build circuits manually when there are EDA tools. Well, although the process can be accomplished easier and faster, sometimes, bringing the expertise of a circuit engineer on the table is recommended; this way, he can thoroughly evaluate the quality of a circuit's system.

Additionally, the operators of EDA tools are selected carefully; usually, they are the ones with a background in the operations of EDA tools and similar equipment. This is due to the expenses, as well as the possible complications, involved in using such devices. In the event that a need for troubleshooting arises, it's best to have somebody who is knowledgeable in circuit designs on standby.

Primary focuses of EDA:

- The presentation of schematic-driven layout

- Advanced and logical interpretation of each circuit component

- Hardware and transistor simulation

XIII.C. - Circuit-Level Optimization

The circuit-level optimization or *power optimization* of EDA tools refers to the various techniques that are employed for the reduction of the total power in a circuit. Although the intent is to modify a circuit's setup economically, the processes shouldn't compromise the product's overall quality. With the main goal of enhancing a circuit's efficiency, the other objectives are to increase speed, eliminate possible leakage, enhance power distribution, and improve functionality.

Circuit-level optimization techniques:

- Modification of voltage scales, thresholds, variables, blocks, supplies, and other voltage-related concerns

- Modification and re-sizing of transistors

- Modification of logic styles

- Re-routing of networks

XIII.D. - Interpretation, Analysis & Verification

Although the automation process of EDA tools may eliminate errors in a circuit's system, a product remains a subject of various testing methods. This is due to the industry of circuitry's insistence on guaranteeing the flawless networks of circuit systems. In the aim of making sure that a circuit's functions are in tune with specific requirements, it is interpreted, analyzed, and verified.

In the event when a circuit (that was created with EDA tools) hadn't undergone tests, there is a likelihood that it won't function for a specific purpose. Especially if the project will be employed for commercial agenda, the industry experts are not granting permission to distribute "unevaluated" circuit systems.

Circuit evaluation methods:

- Assessment of a circuit's maintenance requirements
- Inspection of desired and undesired effects (in relation to mathematical logic)
- Inspection of a circuit's functionality
- Inspection of a circuit's stability
- Verification of physical components
- Verification of static timing

Chapter XIV – The Other Way around: Reverse Engineering

One of the coolest ways of understanding circuits is to disassemble all of its components one by one. First, make sure that it is not connected to any power source. After putting on protective gloves, begin taking apart a component; then, determine its function. Repeat the procedures until you know the purpose of the parts and the importance of having them work as a network.

Now, put them all back together; make sure the circuit works.

Such a process is called *reverse engineering*.

XIV.A. - An Introduction to Reverse Engineering

Reverse engineering, also called *deconstruction, reversing, backwards engineering,* and *back engineering* is the process of extracting knowledge from any device or electronic equipment. It involves the need to deconstruct an entire circuit for further analysis of its components. Although the methods that will be employed are opposite to the process of creation, it is considered as a practical approach of learning circuitry.

Moreover, reverse engineering gives light to Aristotle's concept that the key to understanding the operations of a device is studying each one of its parts. Back in the days, the field is limited to its employment on a circuit and other electronic equipment; now, in the modern world, the application of a "reverse" methodology includes almost anything – from children's toys and household appliances to neuroscience, computer programming, and DNA.

XIV.B. - Reasons for Reversing

One of the privileges that reverse engineering can grant to a circuit creator is the guarantee that a device is made accordingly. In the event that he chooses to base his circuit project on another circuit that was created with *questionable privacy*, he can determine any unethical practices. If he takes apart all of its components, he has the chance to have an insider look; by then, he can confirm whether unregulated modifications are in place.

Why use reverse engineering techniques for circuit-creation:

- Documentation purposes – especially in the case of shortcomings and low-quality circuit documentation, the diagnosis of a circuit is necessary to present new information

- Interfacing – with reverse engineering techniques can be subjected to interfacing; it can be evaluated accordingly, regarding its compatibility with another circuit

- Bug fixing – if there are critical faults in a circuit's design, it can be recognized better with a closer look at each of its components; instead of resorting to assumptions, a circuit creator can identify which part of his project needs modification

- Advanced technical information – advanced technical information is rewarded when opening up a circuit; especially for beginners, reverse engineering is a practical way of learning about the straightforward details within the system

- Incorporation of a new functionality – reverse engineering can allow the incorporation of a feature in a circuit; rather than design another circuit, a circuit creator can simply make modifications on his current project

- Modernization – reversing is beneficial in circuitry since it can be used to modernize a project; for instance, if most modern devices are popular in the market due to an innovative feature, a circuit creator can employ reverse engineering to add the same feature to his circuit

- Guarantee product security – if a circuit creator is unsure of the security of his project, reverse engineering is a way for him to determine certain concerns; he can check the specifications of each component and guarantee that none poses safety risks when put to use

XIV.C. – Is Reverse Engineering Similar to Hacking?

Since it is the method for the extraction of information on a circuit that can't be retrieved ordinarily, reverse engineering is argued to be a form of *corrupt hacking*; it is, therefore, a field that a few others in the electronics industry attempt to avoid. However, for many number of circuit engineers (as well as other engineers), there is brilliance in the entire concept of reverse engineering.

According to those who are not against the field, reverse engineering is a way of outsmarting an already finished product; additionally, as they would insist, isn't the point of engineering exactly that – to build and re-build until satisfying outcome is achieved? It may be considered as a form of hacking, but many contest to the idea that it is behind corrupt objectives.

XIV.D. – The Construction of Reverse Engineered Projects

Inarguably, reverse engineering is rather *destructive* and *invasive*. Some are not in favor of it since they do not welcome the idea of tearing their works apart. For others, however, it is a creative way of improving an already completed project; especially if the particular project is outstanding, they are granted the chance to make it even more outstanding.

Among the common projects that can be modified with the use of reverse engineering are *alarm clock radios, coffee machines,* and *colored lamps.* Alongside, the knowledge of internal systems, they can add a unique functionality that is not included during commercial distribution. For instance, you can add a new beeping sound to an alarm clock radio.

For the construction of various reverse engineering projects, it's advised to have a set of tools handy. Prepare a set of *screwdrivers, magnifiers*, and cutting equipment. Additionally, when the disassembly is completed, have a pack of *electrical tape* nearby.

Reverse engineering project tips for beginners:

- Take pictures of a circuit's front and back system prior to disassembly; you can use it as reference

- List down the set of procedures you plan on following; make sure you adhere to them

XIV.E. - Reverse Engineering & CAD

Reverse engineering rode along with the popularity of *CAD or Computer-Aided Design*. Through the years, the field that used to be limited to the basic improvement of a circuit's system began incorporating complex features. It provides a circuit creator the chance to analyze the internal portion of a device.

Moreover, instead of settling on getting a fundamental view of a circuit project that requires reverse engineering, a circuit creator can meticulously analyze a circuit; he can inspect each component thoroughly and come up at the most practical solution. For its development, circuit engineers, circuit designers, and other professionals on electronics started collaborative works with *architects* and those who are skilled in CAD.

Advantages of using CAD technology for a circuit project:

- To improve the alignment of each circuit component

- To enhance the designation of spaces within a circuit's system

- To modify geometric subjects for boosted performance

- To zoom in (and look closely) on each circuit component

XIV.F. - The Legality of the Industry

In light to the different discussions regarding its similarity to *corrupt hacking*, the reverse engineering industry is subjected to various legal complaints. There are even laws (that usually fall under contract laws and fraudulent manufacturing laws) meant for the protection of all sectors that employ *reversed* circuits or electronic devices.

The term *interoperability* is introduced in relation to a variety of legality concerns. With the emergence of cases that revolve around the disassembly of circuit's parts to compromise the quality of a circuit, some who tackle reverse engineered project are not received well.

Reverse engineering is, therefore, only considered illegal if the primary goal is to achieve interoperability. If the goal is for the improvement of a circuit's overall performance, it is encouraged; along with almost every other means of repairing a system, it is even recommended to arrive at a desired purpose.

Chapter XV – Hacking the System

Different communities of hackers host events that give light to those who are passionate in circuitry.

One community, *Artisan Asylum*, hosts a circuit hacking night once a week. In the gathering, circuit engineering fellows – from beginners to professionals, come together to discuss various concepts in circuitry and electronics. There, like-minded individuals share their love for circuitry and talk about their favorite projects, and basically, anything in the world of circuitry.

Moreover, Artisan Asylum's circuit hacking night provides great learning opportunities for circuit hacking enthusiasts. It presents lessons on how to solder, how to use particular computer programs, and how to modify a circuit to function as desired. Apart from teaching individuals the basics and advanced techniques on how to hack a circuit, and have it work as desired, the community encourages the attendees to think outside of the box and come up with brilliant and innovative ideas.

XV.A. – About Circuit Hacking

Circuit hacking, since it is linked with the word *hacking*, can sometimes be perceived as fraudulent. However, there is nothing fraudulent with it since the main reason why there are circuit hackers is for the improvement or the revision of a project; hacking, in this essence, is defined as the modification of an existing circuit to use it for a different purpose. And, in most cases, a circuit hacker is an individual who exhibits cleverness, open-mindedness, and technical aptness.

Due to a few similar concepts, circuit hacking and reverse engineering are said to be one and the same; they are not. While both may include certain techniques that are intended for the improvement of a circuit's operations, the former is merely focused on developing an existing circuit; it may be invasive, too, but it doesn't involve the *deconstruction of an entire circuit*. Especially if it was determined that the installment of a particular component can achieve a desired functionality, having to tear apart the other sections of a circuit is deemed unnecessary.

Common circuit hacking methods:

- Patching – a simple circuit hacking method that describes identifying a circuit's control mechanism or the most integral part of a circuit. Once the main component is identified, you can install a new and better component

- Component replacement – it is defined as replacing at least one component of a circuit with another component that comes with better quality

XV.B. – A Hacker's Main Tool: FIB Technology

FIB or *Focused Ion Beam* Technology is considered as one of a hacker's main tool since it grants him the chance to hack almost any circuit. Ever since the initial introduction of the applications in the 1990s, their usefulness hadn't come unappreciated. The early versions were not only quite expensive, but also, clearly, in need of improvement; later, the tools underwent continuous modifications from many electronics enthusiasts.

According to a study that was led by the engineers at Berlin Technical University, a person skilled in circuitry can install FIB Technology-based applications to hack into a system's security. For the particular research, an IC with low-level security was the focus; the objective was to work around its level of security with the goal of deliberately eliminating its defensive mechanism. The study was, of course, successful and eventually, it was proven that even high-level tools can be hacked with the same practice. And, as it follows, it sheds light on the concept that *there is no such thing as a tamper-proof circuit.*

Moreover, FIB Technology, as a clever technique of manufacturing, developing, and re-wiring a circuit, has earned the approval of different communities of hackers and circuit engineers. Alongside its advantage of boosting a system's performance, it reduces regular operation time. Due to its ingenious way of allowing an individual who's working on an electronic device to design (and even re-design repeatedly) his project, it was subjected to further developments.

Important parts of applications that incorporate FIB Technology (as shown in the layout):

- Aperture – it is in charge of gathering visual aids, then, modifying these tools for a clear display of retrievable information from a particular electronic device

- Deflector plates – it accepts, interprets, then, measures receivable data; initially, it acknowledges all information prior to the screening of the unnecessary ones

- Extractor – it is in charge of drawing out information from an electronic device, then, transferring them to the hacking mechanism

- Lens – it is in charge of making adjustments to assist when processing information

- Octupoles – it is also known as double quadrupoles or octopoles, which means something that has eight poles; it controls beams of ions

- Suppressor – it is designed to prevent power overload due to voltage spikes; it works by regulating the amount of electric current within a system so a device can remain functional

The installment of FIB Technology can be very promising to a hacker

Functions of applications that incorporate FIB Technology:

- Enable and/or disable intruder detection

- Evaluate a circuit's behavior

- Evaluate a circuit's defects

- Gather secret codes and security keys

- Obtain personal details, sensitive data, and proprietary information

- Remove protection systems (e.g. tamper networks, trace meshes, optical sensors, etc.)

- Route incoming data to be received by another network

- Trace and re-trace changes

XV.C. – Circuit Hacking Project

A plus side to the knowledge of how a circuit operates is that you can choose any from your pack of electronic devices and have it upgraded according to preference; the possibilities of its new functions are endless. You won't even have to spend a grand amount, so long as you're familiar with the functions of particular installments. The result of hacking the original system may be rather bizarre, since the product is no longer the same, but nonetheless, the result is likely the way you desired.

In the sample project below, the goal is hack a charger; particularly, modify an existing charger and have it operate with a battery. It can be connected to any electronic device with a USB port. This is useful during emergencies when an electric outlet is nowhere to be found.

Project example (derived from http://www.maximumpc.com): USB Charger with Battery

A USB charger with battery can be used for hours (depending on your voltage source)

Materials:

- Charger
- 5-volt voltage regulator
- 9-volt battery
- 9-volt battery clip
- Electrical tape

- USB connector

- Copper wire

Procedures (as shown in the layout above):

1. On a side of the charger, drill a hole for the placement of the USB connector.

2. On the other side of the charger, drill a hole for the placement of the 5-volt voltage regulator.

3. At the bottom center (between the 2 holes), place the 9-volt battery.

4. Above it, establish a ground using the copper wire and 9-volt battery clip.

5. Solder the components together.

6. Wrap the product with electrical tape.

Chapter XVI – Advanced Circuit Engineering: Microcontrollers & Robots

Among the plethora of prospects for a circuit engineer is the opportunity to engage in *circuit-bending* or the art (and science) of modifying existing circuits of electronic devices, and turning them into new musical instruments. In many cases, he isn't required to follow a set of rules for *tweaking* a circuit to incorporate a particular sound; in fact, he can re-design an electronic device as desired.

Alongside, an advantage of circuit-bending is its reward of reducing necessary expenses. In the event that he is very resourceful, the circuit creator can maximize the advantage even more; he can install used (but in working condition) components or less costly parts.

Circuit-bending is merely one of the exciting possibilities for a fellow in circuitry. The options are rather limitless, especially if you let your creativity run loose. So long as you are certain that a circuit will work given a particular arrangement, you shouldn't hold back in taking your beginner's knowledge of circuits to an advanced level.

XVI.A. – A Circuit Engineer's Future in Robotics & Computer Engineering

A reward of being skilled in circuitry is the opportunity to venture into other engineering fields such as *robotics engineering* and *computer engineering*. Your knowledge of how a circuit operates? You can look at it from a brand new perspective; you don't have to be simply in the industry of circuit engineering or electronics engineering. Apart from its offer of a more bountiful career; you can employ it to create a project (or a batch of projects) that you can be proud of. With the mastery of the basic circuitry lessons, delving into related fields becomes easier and more exciting.

With your interest in circuitry, you may seek for other career positions; usually, the employers of robotics engineers and computer engineers welcome circuit engineers into their workforce due to *trainability, familiarity with circuits,* and *good background in electronics*. It may take another set of years of studying, along with new skills to learn, but you can definitely go higher; it takes commitment from your end, too.

Advanced lessons that will be useful for a circuit engineer:

- Integral connections for hardware components

- Software and hardware essentials

- Robotic essentials

- Computer operations

- Computer architecture

- Computer programming (recommended programming languages are C and C++)

XVI.B. – Microcontroller + Microcontroller Programming

A *microcontroller* is a small device that serves as the computer in a circuit; it is a common tool that can be found in *remote controls, smart medical assistance equipment, office machines, state-of-the-art appliances,* and *engine control systems.* With the rapid pace of various information-retrieval operations, its function of addressing *size, cost, time,* and *performance* concerns offers privileges a user with improved overall performance. It is usually implanted on a separate electronic device before or after that device is finished. In certain cases, it uses 4-bit words and low frequency clock-rate operations.

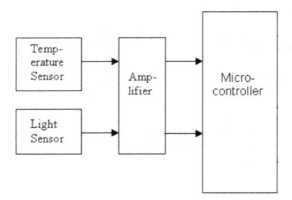

A microcontroller is dependent on a programmer's instructions

Moreover, while a microcontroller is a very useful device, it is only as good as the program that was written for it; this is where the importance of *microcontroller programming* enters the picture. It is a tool that merely executes certain instructions; in the absence of specific commands, it won't function. However, if you design it with even a hundred task capabilities, it can perform each one without fault; granted it was programmed well, it can power a device as desired.

What a microcontroller can do:

- Enable and/or disable clock feature

- Enable and/or disable light capabilities

- Configure audio and video settings

- Add an external monitor

- Automatically detect and/or repair errors

- Automatically update old components

- Magnify an electronic device's performance

- Eliminate unwanted features

- Tighten security features

Example of microcontroller programming:

Result	Microcontroller Programming (in C language)

By tweaking its USB components, a microcontroller's clock setting can be formatted. It is also programmed to activate BL or backlight with a trigger.	for (;;) [
	
	handleserial ();
	
	CDC_USBdevice (&interface)
	
	CDC_USBdevice (&digitalizer)
	
	handleserial ();
	
	]
	
	]
	
	/Setup/ [
	
	int ret
	
	USB_initialize
	
	clock_setup (div1);
	
	BL_off (1), BL_on (0);
	
	ret = digitizer_USB_initialize ();

	if (ret)

XVI.C. – Robots + Robotics

Another way that you can take your knowledge in circuitry up a notch is to consider a career in *robotics engineering*. Due to your familiarity with a circuit, you can begin honing your skills in creating coherent circuits; you can construct a series that is dependent on the individual circuits to deliver its primary function.

As you commit to robotics, like in programming, a lineup of new skills (e.g. artificial intelligence developments, dynamics, motion planning techniques, mapping tactics, etc.) must be acquired, too. This time, other than your hand in circuits and other electronic components, you have to visit aspects in the *mechanical* fields. However, given your exposure to similar concepts in circuitry, learning in the field may not be a challenge.

With your expertise in circuits, you can be behind innovative and extraordinary robotics projects that can be advantageous for both commercial and personal use. It just takes a matter of determination to move forward, and the fact remains that a course in circuit engineering can present you with a satisfying place in robotics, as well as other promising opportunities.

Conclusion

Thank you again for purchasing this book!

I hope this book was able to help you understand the fundamentals in circuit engineering. The lessons shared to you here are meant for a beginner in the subject; the different discussions are written simply. And, so far, it may have dawned on you that there's still more to discover about circuits.

The next step is to learn even more about circuitry and circuit engineering. Especially if you're considering a career in the field, advanced lessons would be good. Since this book has introduced you to the subject, and maybe inspired you to see the fun side in circuits, as well as electronics and electrical engineering, you may want to take the beginner's perspective to a whole other level.

Finally, if you enjoyed this book, please take the time to share your thoughts and post a review on Amazon. It'd be greatly appreciated!

Thank you and good luck!

Book 2
Quality Assurance
By Solis Tech

Software Quality Assurance Made Easy

Quality Assurance: Software Quality Assurance Made Easy

Table Of Contents

Introduction

I want to thank you and congratulate you for purchasing the book, *"Quality Assurance: Software Quality Assurance Made Easy"*.

This book contains proven steps and strategies on how to implement Software Quality Assurance.

Software quality assurance evolved from the quality assurance in industrial production in the 1940s. With the introduction of computers and the development of applications, it has become an important aspect of software development. In this book, you will learn about the various concepts of software quality assurance and its application in your workplace.

Chapter 1 talks about the definitions of software quality assurance and quality control. It is necessary that you understand what it is so that you can fully grasp the other fundamental concepts. Chapter 2 discusses the ways you can implement software quality assurance in an existing environment. In Chapter 3, you will learn how you can ensure that the software produces quality outputs.

Chapter 4 teaches you how to develop and run software testing while Chapter 5 talks about the timing of the software release. In Chapter 6, you will learn about using automated testing tools.

Thanks again for purchasing this book, I hope you enjoy it!

Chapter 1: Definition Of Software Quality Assurance And Software Testing

Software quality assurance is part of the process of software development. It includes the improvement and monitoring of the process. It also follows the processes, procedures, and standards. Furthermore, it ensures the resolution of problems discovered. In effect, it focuses on the prevention of problems.

Software testing, on the other hand, includes the operation of the application or system under controlled conditions, which must include all abnormal and normal conditions. The primary goal of software testing is to know what can go wrong when unexpected and expected scenarios occur. Its focus is on the detection of problems.

Companies differ in assigning responsibilities for quality assurance and software testing. There are organizations that combine both responsibilities to a single person or group. However, it is also common to have various teams that combine developers and testers. Project managers lead such teams. The decision to either combine or separate responsibilities depends on the company's business structure and size. Human beings or machines can perform software testing.

Some projects do not require a group of testers. The need for software testing depends on the project's context and size, the development methodology, the risks, the developers' experience and skill, and other factors. For example, a short-term, low-risk, and small project with expert developers, who know how to use test-first development or thorough unit testing, may not require software test engineers.

In addition, a small or new IT company may not have a dedicated software testing staff even its projects have a need for it. It may outsource software testing or use contractors. It may also adjust its approach on project development and management by using either agile test-first development or more experienced programmers. An inexperienced project manager may use his developers to do their own functional testing or skip thorough testing all together. This decision is highly risky and may cause the project to fail.

If the project is a huge one with non-trivial risks, software testing is important. The use of highly specialized software testers enhances the ability of the project to succeed because different people with different perspectives can offer their invaluable contribution because they have stronger and deeper skills.

In general, a software developer focuses on the technical issues to make a functionality work. On the other hand, a software test engineer focuses on what can go wrong with the functionality. It is very rare to come across a highly

92

effective technical person, who can do both programming and testing tasks. As such, IT companies need software test engineers.

There are various reasons why software may have bugs. First, there is no communication or miscommunication as to the application's requirements. Second, the software is very complex so an inexperienced individual may have a difficult time understanding the software application. In addition, the software may be a big one and includes big databases, data communications, security complexities, different remote and local web services, and multi-tier distributed systems.

Third, there are programming errors. Fourth, the requirements of the software change because the end-user requests for them. In some cases, this end-user may not be aware of the effects of such changes, which can result in errors. The staff's enthusiasm is affected. Continuous modification requirements are a reality. Quality assurance and software test engineers must be able to plan and adapt continuous testing to prevent bugs from affecting the software.

Fifth, time pressures can be difficult to manage. Mistakes often occur during crunch times. Sixth, people involved in the project may not be able to manage their own egos. Seventh, the code has poor documentation or design. It is difficult to modify and maintain codes that are poorly written or documented. Bugs can occur if IT companies do not offer incentives for developers to write maintainable, understandable, and clear codes. Most companies offer incentives when they are able to finish the code quickly. Eighth, the use of software development tools can also result to bugs.

How Quality Assurance Evolved

In 1946, the US Occupation Forces established the Quality Movement in Japan. The movement follows the research of W. Edwards Deming and the Statistical Process Control papers. The methods discussed by the research and papers pertained to industrial production. Each process of production has an output with a required specification and a verifiable main product. The Quality Control group measures the output at different production stages. It ensures that the output falls within the acceptable variances.

The Quality Assurance group does not part in the production process. It audits the process to ensure compliance with the established standards and guidelines. It gives its input for the continuous improvement of the process. In a manufacturing setup, it is easy to differentiate between quality assurance and quality control. These methods become the norm in manufacturing. Since they work in industrial production, they spawned the birth of software quality control and software quality assurance.

Quality Attributes Of Software

Hewlett Packard's Robert Grady developed the common definition of the Software Quality Attributes. The FURPS model identified the following characteristics: functionality, usability, reliability, performance, and supportability (FURPS).

The functional attributes pertain to the features of the software. They answer the question about the purpose of the software instead of its use. The reason for the software's existence is different from the concerns about its reliability, look and feel, and security. The usability attributes are characteristics pertaining to user interface issues like consistency, interface aesthetics, and accessibility.

The reliability attributes include recoverability, accuracy, and availability of the system while performance attributes pertain to issues like startup time, recovery time, system response time, and information throughput. Supportability addresses issues like localizability, scalability, installation, configurability, compatibility, maintainability, adaptability, and testability. The FURPS model evolved into FURPS+ to include specification of constraints like physical, interface, implementation, and design constraints.

The Software Quality Control team tests the quality characteristics. The tests for usability and functionality occur during execution of the actual software. On the other hand, adaptability and supportability tests occur through code inspection. It is not the responsibility of the Software Quality Control or Software Quality Assurance to put the quality attributes into the software. The Software Quality Control team tests for the absence or presence of such characteristics while the Software Quality Assurance group ensures that each stakeholder follow the right standards and procedures during software execution.

In theory, the implementation of FURPS+ will overcome the problems caused by the software's intangible nature because the Software Quality Control team can measure each software attribute. For example, the amount of time it takes for programmers to fix a bug is a measure of supportability. To improve it requires the implementation of new coding standards.

The Software Quality Control group can inspect the code to ensure compliance with the coding standard while the Software Quality Assurance team can ensure that the quality control and programmer teams follow the right standards and process. It is the duty of the Software Quality Assurance group to collect and analyze the time spent on fixing the bug so that it can provide an input in terms of its usefulness to the process improvement initiative.

Chapter 2: Introducing Software Quality Assurance Procedures To An Existing Company

The introduction of the software quality assurance procedures rely on the risks involved and the company's size. If the organization is large and the projects are high-risk, the management must consider a more formal quality assurance process. On the other hand, if the risk is lower, the implementation of quality assurance may be a step-at-a-time procedure. The processes of quality assurance maintain balance with productivity.

If the project or the company is small, an ad-hoc process may be more appropriate. The success of the software development relies on the team leaders and developers. More importantly, there must be enough communications between software testers, managers, customers, and developers. Requirement specifications must be complete, testable, and clear. There must be procedures for design and code reviews, as well as retrospectives. Common approaches used are Agile, Kaizen, and Deming-Shewhart Plan-Do-Check-Act methods.

It is important to evaluate documents, code, specifications, plans, and requirements. To do this, it is necessary to prepare issues lists, checklists, inspection meetings, and walkthroughs. This process is what IT people refer to as verification. On the other hand, validation occurs after verification and includes actual testing of the application. A walkthrough is evaluation in an informal meeting. There is no need to prepare for it.

An inspection is more formal than a walkthrough and attended by at most eight people including a reader, a recorder, and a moderator. Usually, an inspection's subject is a test plan or requirements specification so that the attendees will know the software's problems. The attendees must read the document before attending an inspection so they will find the problems prior to the meeting. It is difficult to prepare for an inspection but it is an effective and least costly way to ensure quality.

Testing Requirements That Must Be Considered

The basis of black box testing is the software's functionality and requirements. A software tester need not be knowledgeable of code or internal design. White box testing, on the other hand, requires knowledge of code. It takes into consideration the code statements, paths, branches, and conditions. Unit testing requires testing of particular code modules or functions. Usually, the application developer performs it because it requires detailed knowledge of the code and program design.

API testing is testing of data exchange or messaging among systems parts. An incremental integration testing tests the application when there is a new functionality, which must be independent to work separately before it can be included in the application. The application programmer or software tester performs this type of testing. An integration testing requires the testing of the various parts of the software in order to know if they work together properly. Functional testing, on the other hand, is a kind of black box testing that focuses on the application's functional requirements. The software testers perform it.

System testing is also another type of black box testing. It includes testing of the general requirements specifications and all the various parts of the software. End-to-end testing, on the other hand, is a macro type of system testing. It includes testing the whole software in various situations that replicates real-world use. Smoke testing or sanity testing is an initial testing to know if the new version is performing well so that major testing can commence. Regression testing retests the application after some modifications or fixes.

Acceptance testing is final testing the software based on customer's specifications. Load testing is software testing under heavy loads in order to find out when the response time of the system fails or degrades. Stress testing, on the other hand, is system functional testing with unusually heavy loads, large complex queries of the database, using large numerical values, and heavy repetition of certain inputs or actions. Performance testing is testing using test or quality assurance plans.

The goal of usability testing depends on the customer or end-user. It uses techniques like surveys, user interviews, and user sessions' video recording. Software testers and developers are not the people to implement usability testing. Install/uninstall testing uses processes to test upgrade, full, or partial install/uninstall of the software. Recovery testing determines how the software can recover in catastrophic instances like hardware failures and crashes. Failover testing is another name for recovery testing.

Security testing tests how the application protects against willful damage, unauthorized access, and the likes. It uses sophisticated testing methods. Compatibility testing tests how the application performs in some environments. Exploratory testing, on the other hand, is an informal and creative testing that does not use any formal test cases or plans. Usually, software testers are new to the application. Ad-hoc testing is almost the same as exploratory testing but the software testers understand the application prior to testing.

Context-driven testing focuses on the software's intended use, culture, and environment. For example, medical equipment software has a different testing approach than a computer game. User acceptance testing determines if the application is satisfactory to the customer or end-user. Comparison testing, on the other hand, compares the software with its competitors.

Alpha testing occurs when the software is almost finished. Usually, end users perform this type of testing. Beta testing is testing when the software is finished and ready for final release. Like alpha testing, this kind of testing is for end users. Finally, mutation testing uses test cases and allows for code changes and retesting using the original test cases to discover software bugs.

Common Problems And Solutions In Developing Software

Software development can encounter common problems like poor user stories or requirements, unrealistic schedule, inadequate testing, featuritis, and miscommunication. Problems can arise if there requirements are incomplete, unclear, not testable, or too general. Furthermore, if the software development has a short timetable, problems can also be evident. If the software does not pass through the testing process, the IT organization will only know of problems if the system crashes or the end users complain.

In addition, problems can arise if the users or customers request for more new functionalities even after the development goals are set. Finally, if there is miscommunication between the programmers and customers, problems are inevitable. If it is an agile project, the problems become evident when it strays away from agile principles.

If there are common problem then there are also common solutions like solid requirements, realistic schedules, adequate testing, sticking to original requirements, and communication. Software requirements must be complete, clear, cohesive, detailed, testable, and attainable. All players concerned must agree upon them. In agile environments, there must be close coordination with end users or customers so that any change in requirement is clear. There must be enough time for design, planning, bug fixing, testing, changes, retesting, and documentation. Each person must not feel burnout during the project.

For testing to be adequate, it must start early. Retesting must occur after each change or fix. There must be enough time for bug fixing and testing. If the end user or customer requests for excessive changes when development has begun, it is important that the project manager explain the consequences. If the change is important, a schedule change is inevitable to accommodate it.

The project manager must manage the expectations of the end users or customer. In an agile environment, the project manager can expect significant change in the initial requirements. There must be a schedule for inspections and walkthroughs. The use of communication tools is important to ensure cooperation and teamwork.

Software Quality Assurance And Software Quality Control In The Workplace

If there is no formal implementation of Software Quality Assurance/Software Quality Control, the quality group can mirror that of an engineering services group. It performs the tasks not done by the development team. It reports to the application development manager. Under this scenario, the manager can instruct the quality assurance personnel to install a load-testing tool and declare him as a performance expert. Although the quality assurance person must perform load testing, it is the job of the software designer/programmer. As such, the software quality assurance/software quality control must be separate from the development team.

Software quality assurance requires the establishment of templates used during reviews. Such templates must have sections for both non-functional and functional requirements. For example, the requirements for performance must be in terms of transaction rates and user population. The use of Traceability Matrix can help in the requirements management. The matrix also encourages the analyst to use individual requirements for cross-referencing.

Software quality assurance verifies that the requirements comply with the templates and that they are not ambiguous. It reviews the risks of non-completion of the non-functional attributes, as well as the Traceability Matrix, to ensure usability of all requirements in other specifications. Software quality assurance can write the test cases, which refer to some of the requirements. It can cross-reference the requirements in the Traceability Matrix.

The interface specification is a requirement if the software is component-based. Software quality assurance must subject the document to verification. It must also subject other lower level specifications to quality assurance if such requirements are critical. Even if there are limited resources for software quality assurance, an IT organization can obtain a good return-on-investment if it pays attention to requirements and interfaces.

Chapter 3: Ensuring Software Quality

Software quality is the delivery of bug-free software within budget and on time. Because quality is subjective, it depends on the customer and his overall influence in the project. A customer can be an end user, a customer contract officer, a customer acceptance tester, a customer manager, a software maintenance engineer, and others. Each customer has his own definition of quality.

A code is good if it works, is secure, bug free, maintainable, and readable. Some companies have standards, which their programmers follow. However, each developer has his own idea about what is best. Standards have different metrics and theories. If there are excessive rules and standards, they can limit creativity and productivity. A design can be functional or internal design.

An internal design is good if the overall structure of the software code is clear, easily modifiable, understandable, and maintainable. It is robust with the capability to log status and with sufficient error handling. Furthermore, the software works as expected. A functional design is good if the software functionality comes from the requirements of the end user and customer. Even an inexperienced user can use the software without reading the user manual or seeking online help.

The software life cycle starts with the conception of the application and commences when the software is no longer used. It includes factors like requirements analysis, initial concept, internal design, functional design, test planning, documentation planning, document preparation, coding, maintenance, testing, integration, retesting, updates, and phase out.

A good software test engineer must possess a test to break attitude, which means that he must be able to focus on the detail in order to ensure that the application is of good quality. He must be diplomatic and tactful so that he can maintain a good relationship with the programmers, the customers, and the managements.

It is helpful if he has previous experience on software development so that he understands the whole process deeply. A good software test engineer is able to appreciate the point of view of the programmers. He must have good judgment skills to be able to determine critical or high-risk application areas that require testing.

A good quality assurance engineer also shares the same qualities with a good software test engineer. Furthermore, he must understand the whole process of software development and the organizations' goals and business approach. He must possess understanding of all sides of issues in order to communicate effectively with everyone concerned. He must be diplomatic and patient, especially in the early stages of the quality assurance process. Lastly, he must be able to detect problems during inspections and reviews.

Qualities Of A Good Quality Assurance Or Test Manager

A good manager must be familiar with the process of software development and must be enthusiastic and promote positivity in the team. He must be able to increase productivity by promoting teamwork and cooperation between quality assurance, software, and test engineers. If the processes require improvements, he must be diplomatic in ensuring smooth implementation of such changes.

He must be able to withstand pressure and offer the right feedback about quality issues to the other managers. He must be able to hire and keep the right personnel. He must possess strong communication skills to deal with everyone concerned in the process. Lastly, he must stay focused and be able to hold meetings.

Importance Of Documentation In Quality Assurance

If the team is large, it is more useful to have the proper documentation for efficient communication and management of projects. Documentation of quality assurance practices is necessary for repeatability. Designs, specifications, configurations, business rules, test plans, code changes, bug reports, test cases, and user manuals must have proper documentation. A system of documentation is necessary for easy obtaining and finding of information.

Each project has its own requirements. If it is an agile project, the requirements may change and evolve. Thus, there is no need for detailed documentation. However, it is useful to document user stories. Documentation on the software requirements describes the functionality and properties of the software. It must be clear, reasonably detailed, complete, attainable, cohesive, and testable. It may be difficult to organize and determine the details but there are tools and methods that are available.

It is important to exercise care in documenting the requirements of the project's customer, who may be an outside or in-house personnel, an end user, a customer contract officer, a customer acceptance tester, a customer manager, a sales person, or a software maintenance engineer. If the project did not meet the expectations, any of these customers can slow down the project.

Each organization has its own way of handling requirements. If the project is an agile project, the requirements are in the user stories. On the other hand, for other projects, the requirements are in the document. Some organizations may use functional specification and high-level project plans. In every requirement, documentation is important to help software testers to make test plans and perform testing. Without any significant documentation, it is impossible to determine if the application meets the user expectations.

Even if the requirements are not testable, it is still important to test the software. The test results must be oriented towards providing information about the risk levels and the status of the application. It is significant to have the correct testing approach to ensure success of the project. In an agile project, various approaches can use methods that require close cooperation and interaction among stakeholders.

Chapter 4: How To Develop And Run Software Testing

To develop the steps for software testing, it is necessary to consider the following.

First, it is important to get the requirements, user stories, internal design, functional design, and any other information that can help with the testing process.

Second, testing must have budget and schedule.

Third, it must have personnel with clear responsibilities.

Fourth, there must be project context to determine testing approaches, scope, and methods.

Fifth, identification of limitations and scope of tests is necessary in order to set priorities.

Sixth, testing must include methods and approaches applicable.

Seventh, it must have the requirements to determine the test environment.

Eighth, it must have requirements for testing tools.

Ninth, it is important to determine the data requirements for testing input.

Tenth, identification of labor requirements and tasks are important.

Eleventh, it must determine milestones, timelines, and schedule estimates.

Twelfth, testing must include error classes, boundary value analysis, and input equivalence classes, when needed.

Thirteenth, it must have a test plan and documents for approvals and reviews.

Fourteenth, testing must determine test scenarios and cases.

Fifteenth, it must include reviews, approvals of test cases, inspections, approaches, and scenarios.

Sixteenth, there must be testing tools and test environment, user manuals, configuration guides, reference documents, installation guides, test tracking processes, archiving and logging processes, and test input data.

Seventeenth, it must include software releases,

The Test Plan

A test plan is a document, which includes scope, objectives, and focus of the software testing activity. To prepare it, it is important to consider the efforts needed to validate the software's acceptability. The test plan must help even those people who are not part of the test group. Testing must be thorough but not very detailed.

The test plan can include the following: the title, the software version number, the plan's revision history, table of contents, the intended audience, the goal of testing, the overview of the software, relevant documents, legal or standards requirements, identifier and naming standards, and requirements for traceability. The test plan must also include overall project organization, test organization, dependencies and assumptions, risk analysis of the project, focus and priorities of testing, limitations and scope, test outline, data input outline, test environment, analysis of test environment validity, configuration and setup of test environment, and processes for software migration among other things.

A test case includes the input, event, or action plus its expected result in order to know if software's functionality is working as planned. It contains test case identifier, objective, test case name, test setup, requirements for input data, steps, and expected results. The details may differ, depending on the project context and organization. Some organizations handle test cases differently. Most of them use less-detailed test scenarios for simplicity and adaptability of test documentation. It is important to develop test cases because it is possible to detect problems and errors in the software through them.

When A Bug Is Discovered

If the software has a bug, the programmers must fix it. The software must undergo retesting after the resolution of the error. Regression testing must be able to check that the solutions performed were not able to create more problems within the application. A system for problem tracking must be set up so it becomes easier to perform the retesting. There are various software tools available to help the quality assurance team.

In tracking the problems, it is good to consider the following: complete information about the bug, bug identifier, present bug status, software version number, how the bug was discovered, specifics about environment and hardware, test case information, bug description, cause of the bug, fix description, retesting results, etc. There must be a reporting process so that the appropriate personnel will know about the errors and fixes.

A configuration management includes the various processes used to coordinate, control, and track requirements, code, problems, documentation, designs, change requests, tools, changes made, and person who made the changes. If the software has many bugs, the software tester must report them and focus on critical bugs. Because this problem can affect the schedule, the software tester must inform the managers and send documentation in order to substantiate the problem.

The decision to stop testing is difficult to do, especially for complex applications. In some cases, complete testing is not possible. Usually, the decision to stop testing considers the deadlines, the degree of test cases completion, the depletion of the test budget, the specified coverage of code, the reduction of the bug rate, and the ending of alpha or beta testing periods. If there is not enough time to perform thorough testing, it is important to focus the testing on important matters based on risk analysis. If the project is small, the testing can depend on risk analysis again.

In some cases, there are organizations that are not serious about quality assurance. For them, it is important to solve problems rather than prevent problems. Problems regarding software quality may not be evident. Furthermore, some organizations reward people who fix problems instead of incentivizing prevention of problems. Risk management includes actions that prevent things from happening. It is a shared responsibility among stakeholders. However, there must be a point person who is primarily responsible for it. In most cases, the responsibility falls on the quality assurance personnel.

Chapter 5: Deciding When To Release The Software To Users

In most projects, the decision to release the software depends on the timing of the end testing. However, for most applications, it is difficult to specify the release criteria without using subjectivity and assumptions. If the basis of the release criteria is the result of a specific test, there is an assumption that this test has addressed all the necessary software risks.

For many projects, this is impossible to do without incurring huge expenses. Therefore, the decision is actually a leap of faith. Furthermore, most projects try to balance cost, timeliness, and quality. As such, testing cannot address the balance of such factors when there is a need to decide on the release date.

Usually, the quality assurance or test manager decides when to release the software. However, this decision involves various assumptions. First, the test manager understands the considerations, which are significant in determining the quality of the software to justify release. Second, the quality of the software may not balance with cost and timeliness. In most organization, there is not enough definition for sufficient quality. Thus, it becomes very subjective and may vary from day to day or project to project.

The release criteria must consider the sales goals, deadlines, market considerations, legal requirements, quality norms of the business segment, programming and technical considerations, expectations of end users, internal budget, impact on the other projects, and a host of other factors. Usually, the project manager must know all these factors.

Because of the various considerations, it may not be possible for the quality assurance manager or test manager to decide the release of the software. However, he may be responsible in providing inputs to the project manager, who makes the release decision. If the project or the organization is small, the decision to release the software rests on the project manager or the product manager. For larger organizations or projects, there must be a committee to decide when to release the software.

If the software requirements change continuously, it is important for all stakeholders to cooperate from the beginning so that they all understand how the change in requirements may affect the project. They may decide on alternate strategies and test plans in advance. It is also beneficial to the project if the initial design of the software can accommodate changes later on. A well-documented code makes it easier for programmers to make the necessary changes.

It is also good to use rapid prototyping if possible so that customers will not make more requests for changes because they are sure of their requirements from the very beginning. The initial schedule of the project must allow extra lead-time for these changes. If possible, all changes must be in the "Phase 2" of the software version. It is important that only easily implemented requirements must be in the project.

The difficult ones must be in the future versions. The management and the customers must know about costs, inherent risks, and scheduling impacts of big changes in the requirements. If they know about the challenges, they can decide whether to continue with the changes or not.

There must be balance between expected efforts with the effort to set up automated testing for the changes. The design of the automated test scripts must be flexible. Its focus must be on aspects of application, which will remain unchanged. The reduction of the appropriate effort for the risk analysis of the changes can be through regression testing.

The design of the test cases must be flexible. The focus must be on ad-hoc testing and not on detailed test cases and test plans. If there is a continuous request for changes in the requirements, it is unreasonable to expect that requirements will remain stable and pre-determined. Thus, it may be appropriate to use approaches for agile development.

It is difficult to determine if software has significant hidden or unexpected functionality. It also indicates that the software development process has deeper problems. The functionality must be removed if does not serve any purpose to the software because it may have unknown dependencies or impacts. If not removed, there must be a consideration for the determination of regression testing needs and risks. The management must know if there are significant risks caused by the unexpected functionality.

The implementation of quality assurance processes is slow over time because the stakeholders must have a consensus. There must be an alignment of processes and organizational goals. As the organization matures, there will be an improvement on productivity. Problem prevention will be the focus. There will be a reduction of burnout and panics. There will be less wasted effort and more improved focus.

The processes must be efficient and simple to prevent any "Process Police" mentality. Furthermore, quality assurance processes promote automated reporting and tracking thereby minimizing paperwork. However, in the short run, implementation may be slow. There will be more days for inspections, reviews, and planning but less time for handling angry end users and late night fixing of errors.

If the growth of the IT organization is very rapid, fixed quality assurance processes may be impossible. Thus, it is important to hire experienced people. The management must prioritize issues about quality and maintain a good relationship with the customers. Every employee must know what quality means to the end user.

Chapter 6: Using Automated Testing Tools

If the project is small, learning and implementing the automated testing tools may not be worth it. However, these automated testing tools are important for large projects. These tools use a standard coding language like Java, ruby, python, or other proprietary scripting language. In some cases, it is necessary to record the first tests for the generation of the test scripts. Automated testing is challenging if there are continuous changes to the software because a change in test code is necessary every time there is a new requirement. In addition, the analysis and interpretation of results can be difficult.

Data driven or keyword driven testing is common in functional testing. The maintenance of actions and data is easy through a spreadsheet. The test drivers read the information for them to perform the required tests. This strategy provides more control, documentation, development, and maintenance of test cases. Automated tools can include code analyzers, coverage analyzers, memory analyzers, load/performance test tools, web test tools, and other tools.

A test engineer, who does manual testing, determines if the application performs as expected. He must be able to judge the expected outcome. However, in an automated test, the computer judges the test outcome. A mechanism must be present for the computer to compare automatically between the actual and expected outcomes for every test scenario. If the test engineer is new to automated testing, it is important that he undergo training first.

Proper planning and analysis are important in selecting and using an automated tool for testing. The right tool must be able to test more thoroughly than manual methods. It must test faster and allow continuous integration. It must also reduce the tedious manual testing. The automation of testing is costly. However, it may be able to provide savings in the long term.

Choosing The Appropriate Test Environment

There is always a tradeoff between cost and test environment. The ultimate scenario is to have a collection of test environments, which mirror exactly all possible usage, data, network, software, and hardware characteristics that the software can use. For most software, it is impossible to predict all environment variations. Furthermore, for complex and large systems, it is extremely expensive to duplicate a live environment.

The reality is that decisions on the software environment characteristics are important. Furthermore, the choice of test environments takes into consideration logistical, budget, and time constraints. People with the most technical experience and knowledge, as well as with the deep understanding of constraints and risks, make these decisions. If the project is low risk or small, it is common to take the informal approach. However, for high risk or large projects, it is important to take a more formalize procedure with many personnel.

It is also possible to coordinate internal testing with efforts for beta testing. In addition, it is possible to create built-in automated tests upon software installation by users. The tests are able to report information through the internet about problems and application environment encountered. Lastly, it is possible to use virtual environments.

The Best Approach To Test Estimation

It is not easy to find the best approach because it depends on the IT organization, the project, as well as the experience of the people involved. If there are two projects with the same size and complexity, the right test effort for life-critical medical software may be very large compared to a project involving an inexpensive computer game. The choice of a test estimation approach based on complexity and size may be applicable to a project but not to the other one.

The implicit risk context approach caters to a quality assurance manager or project manager, who uses risk context with past personal experiences to allocate resources for testing. The risk context assumes that each project is similar to the others. It is an experience-based intuitive guess.

The metrics-based approach, on the other hand, uses past experiences on different projects. If there is already data from a number of projects, the information is beneficial in future test planning. For each new project, the basis of adjustment of required test time is the available metrics. In essence, this is not easy to do because it is judgment based on historical experience.

The test-work breakdown approach decomposes the testing tasks into smaller tasks to estimate testing with a reasonable accuracy. It assumes that the breakdown of testing tasks is predictable and accurate and that it is feasible to estimate the testing effort. If the project is large, this is not feasible because there is a need to extend testing time if there are many bugs. In addition to, there is a need to extend development time.

The iterative approach is for large test projects. An initial rough estimate is necessary prior to testing. Once testing begins and after finishing a small percentage of testing work, there is a need to update the testing estimate because testers have already obtained additional knowledge of the issues, risks, and software quality. There is also a need to update test schedules and plans. After finishing a larger percentage of testing work, the testing estimate requires another update. The cycle continues until testing ends.

The percentage-of-development approach requires a quick way of testing estimation. If the project has 1,000 hours of estimated programming effort, the

IT firm usually assigns a 40% ratio for testing. Therefore, it will allot 400 hours for testing. The usefulness of this approach depends on risk, software type, personnel, and complexity level.

In an agile software development approach, the test estimate is unnecessary if the project uses pure test-driven development although it is common to mix some automated unit tests with either automated or manual functional testing. By the nature of agile-based projects, they are not dependent on testing efforts but on the construction of the software.

Conclusion

Thank you again for purchasing this book!

I hope this book was able to help you to understand the concepts of Software Quality Assurance.

The next step is to apply what you learned from this book to your work.

Finally, if you enjoyed this book, please take the time to share your thoughts and post a review on Amazon. It'd be greatly appreciated!

Thank you and good luck!

www.ingramcontent.com/pod-product-compliance
Lightning Source LLC
Chambersburg PA
CBHW071229050326
40689CB00011B/2503